Lady, Will You Hear Me?

True Ghost Story

Susan E. Rogers

Published by Susan E. Rogers, 2024.

While every precaution has been taken in the preparation of this book, the publisher assumes no responsibility for errors or omissions, or for damages resulting from the use of the information contained herein.

LADY, WILL YOU HEAR ME?

First edition. August 22, 2024.

ISBN: 979-8227059932

Written by Susan E. Rogers.

Table of Contents

For Hardy, my greatest fan

Who always believes, understands, and encourages

Introduction

Spirits are the residual energy of those who once lived but have passed on to another realm after death. Their soul never dies. Its energy allows them to communicate with those who are still alive and open to them.

I am a psychic and a medium. I see and talk to the ghosts of dead people.

Spirits have been around me since I was a child. I never realized then that it was anything special. I remembered dreams, visions, and conversations with invisible friends. As I got older, my understanding of my abilities matured and so did my realization that this was something special, and different. Like most intuitives, survival in the guise of normalcy was a lesson learned early. Our culture never readily accepts psychics, and those so gifted do well to keep a low profile.

I wasn't afraid of these Spirits, but I came to recognize that I wasn't supposed to talk about them to anyone else. My gift stayed hidden for most of my adult life. At the time of my divorce and subsequent independence, I made the decision to cultivate my psychic ability for my own well-being and for others in need of help and guidance.

Why do Spirits come to me? I believe it's because I can hear them and because I listen to them. They tell me their stories filled with sadness, trauma, grief, and isolation. I never judge them. I offer kindness and compassion, help them heal and move on. It's the best answer I have for that question. I search for them in an attempt to validate the circumstances and events of their lives. Sometimes I'm successful, other times I'm not.

Once I listen and understand their stories, the Spirits want me to share it with people who were important to them personally or with others who might have undergone a similar experience. There's a purpose to their communication, beyond clearing and healing their own souls.

I'm in awe of these Spirits. Some of them experienced horrific situations and some passed because of a traumatic event. They continue to suffer after death, as they relive the anguish and sorrow that so deeply impacted their lives. Yet, they have to be courageous and resolute to make the effort to return to the physical realm and make contact with a living person.

I believe there's another reason these Spirits contact me. They don't want to be forgotten. We, the currently living, can look at photographs of our deceased loved ones. The memories fade quickly, however, after a generation or two. How often have we looked at old photos without any identification and wondered just who those people were, captured at that moment in time? We can visit a family gravestone in a cemetery. Have you looked around at the older stones, damaged and untended, and wonder if anyone thinks about them anymore? Once I know these Spirits and their history, I write their stories for others to read. They become alive again in the minds and memories of the living. This is important to them and should be to us.

I'm grateful for the contact from Spirits. Once I hear their story and place them in context with my research, they become special friends to me. When their story's been told and they're released from the trauma and stress they carried forward from their physical lives, they can move on and are gone. I miss them and their presence.

There's always new contact from other Spirits. I feel their energy around me wherever I am, but I don't always receive a message. When they do attempt to communicate, and I sense no mal-intent, I welcome them into my life. Spirits have something to teach me, and I'm always ready to help however I can. This has become a normal part of my life and I wouldn't change it or have it any other way.

Lady, Will You Hear Me?
A True Ghost Story

. . . .

The horror of war, any war, creates powerful emotional energy that never truly dissipates. Combined with the violent energy of suicide, the resulting force can propel a spirit into absolute disarray. The usual confusion and disconnection a soul experiences when crossing over to the afterlife escalates exponentially when such a potent catalyst propels it into the Spirit realm.

But what if the powerful trauma-infused energy of two souls who underwent these intense, violent conditions were to collide? How can a ghost be expected to remember everything correctly after such a cataclysmic upheaval?

Part I – The Story

1

The Reiki Session And First Contact

Lady, will you hear me?

I am very much alone and have no one to speak with. I must tell of horrific events, of what happened to me, and to them. And then of what happened to me alone. I have found you here before and know that you are powerful and open to my kind. Please, you must hear me, so I may unburden my soul.

The ghost of Joe Tripp asked for my help during a Reiki session.

Once a month a group of us met at the wellness center owned by my friend and mentor Cherie to practice Reiki with each other. As a very simple explanation, Reiki is a Japanese healing technique that can provide stress relief and relaxation while promoting healing. It's a holistic method, using the body's own life force energy to support the whole person physically, emotionally, mentally, and spiritually.

The Reiki practitioner administers treatment by placing their hands at strategic points on the body and channeling energy. These Chakra points, which are the body's centers of spiritual power, help to regulate the body's functions. There are seven primary Chakras from the base of the spine to the crown of the head and each governs a specific area of the person's well-being. It's not my intent to give instruction about Reiki or the Chakras here, only to illustrate how my psychic ability can work at times.

I earned a Reiki Master Teacher Certificate in May 2013. Ghosts and spirits regularly communicated messages to me during sessions, both when I received and when I practiced on someone else. Frequently, these were the spirits of people who died and passed beyond this life. Just as often, I received messages or images from a past life of the person I was providing Reiki treatment to, or from spirit guides who were once living people in one of the individual's past lives.

That night, it was Donna's turn on the table first. I worked between her solar plexus and the root Chakra at the base of her spine. Soon after I started, I felt an uncomfortable physical sensation like someone stuck the end of a stick in my mouth and pushed it against the back of my throat. It's possible to take on the physical sensations or emotions of the Reiki recipient during a session, but generally they're brief and serve to focus the healing energy where it's needed most.

This sensation wouldn't go away, no matter what I did or thought. With my hands on Donna's Chakra, I felt incredible amounts of energy, heat, and vibration. These feelings were overwhelmingly strong, the indication of powerful emotional energy being channeled through to me. I wondered if there was something more going on than only the energy being released from her.

Lynn was next, and I worked in the same area. The sensation of the stick in my throat persisted. Not only did the feeling continue, it became more and more irritating and uncomfortable, almost painful. The strong emotional charges continued as well, and I could barely concentrate. These sensations indicated a psychic message trying to get through to me.

Toward the end of Lynn's session, I sensed something else. The energy coming through to me wasn't just from Reiki. I felt a push against me, an actual physical push, against the side of my body first and then against my torso. I worked hard to keep my balance, but the impact was strong against me. Now I was convinced there was another being or ghost who was determined to get my attention.

Mentally, I commanded the spirit to identify itself and tell me its purpose. I received no answer, though I asked several times. Despite the silence, I sensed terrible loss and anguish emanating from the ghost. At one point I received such an overwhelming feeling of sorrow that I knew it was a plea for my help. I couldn't and wouldn't turn away.

I asked my friends if I could take my turn next on the table. I explained there was a spirit trying to make contact with me and it needed the energy of the Reiki session to come through completely. I didn't say anything about the feeling in my throat as I stretched out on the table and tried to relax. As the others began my Reiki session, I felt the spirit's presence with me, sad and troubled as he began to speak. He told his story and I didn't interrupt him.

I wrote this spirit's story in a narrative form, to make it easier to read and understand. The original communication was relayed to me in thoughts and images that I followed in sequence. I tried as much as possible to maintain the voice, tone, and language he used as he related the story to me in one continuous message. This is the story as he told it to me...

2

Joe Tripp Tells His Civil War Story

My name is Joe. Or rather, I was Joe Tripp. I was almost nineteen, barely out of boyhood, a strong and haughty young man, and I was proud to do what I saw fit as my duty by our country. I signed up right away to fight in the war with the Rebels. My father was pleased but not my Ma. She fretted and fussed, afraid that I'd not be coming back, you see. I paid her no mind, really, or at least I tried not to. She carried on so it was enough to rattle any man's nerve a bit.

Off I went anyway, just like the other boys I knew from town. We all signed up and they gave us a uniform and a kit. I already had my musket that I brought along with me. Before this it was only used for shooting small critters – possum, rabbits and the like. I didn't even think that now I was supposed to use it to kill another man.

I dread to think of it even after this long time. At first it seemed an adventure. I was never before any farther in this country than the great city of New Bedford. But it didn't take long until it stopped being excitement and became a ceaseless nightmare. We marched from place to place all over countryside I never heard of, much less wanted to see. There wasn't a day gone by that I wasn't sore and dirty and hungry, and if truth be told, afraid too. And I was tired, bone tired. The only time we stopped to rest was before we got ready to fight.

That was a terrible sight. We all lined up, in the mud or in the briars or whatever was there. Some of us stood and some of us kneeled, and all of us aimed our guns. But Lord, what we aimed at! Other men and boys, just like ourselves. I saw the tiredness and the fear in their eyes, too. We were that close. Then the Lieutenant yelled the order and we pulled the triggers. We had to shoot at them, those other soldiers lined up there. Just like us. They said that was what we had to do. That's what we signed up to do – kill them to save our country and free the slaves. Fight those men and kill them dead, before they killed us.

After a while you didn't think, because thinking hurt too much. It hurt in my head and in my gut and in my heart. And the noise, the relentless bang of the guns, the teeth-knocking boom of cannons, and the ear-piercing screams of men hit with shot or bullets, burning-hot pieces of iron searing their way through flesh and bone. Men I saw in front of me, only yards away, fell on the ground next to their comrades. But worse, men who stood next to me one minute and then suddenly writhed on the ground right at my feet, the blood pouring out of them as they screamed and moaned. The moaning was worse, begging for help that none of us could stop to give or we'd end up on the ground dying right next to them.

Then one day the worst happened. It was Charlie. One minute he stood by my side, firing away with that old musket of his, and then he was gone. At first I thought he ran. We talked sometimes, when we were supposed to sleep, but the noise, still in our ears after many days passing, kept us awake. We shared our fears to keep ourselves as whole as could be. We thought it would be glorious to fight for our country. We soon both knew there was no glory, only agony.

How could Charlie run and leave me behind? I ducked, intended to turn around to see his tail end. Instead I slipped in the gore on the ground around me and fell on top of somebody. No, not somebody – Charlie. Oh Lord, it was Charlie! There was a hole straight on in the center of his forehead, a bullet hole like another eye. All three of those eyes wide open and looking straight at me. I screamed then but no noise came out. I couldn't move.

I don't know how long I lay there on the ground, but they must have thought I was dead too. When I came to, the battle was done and it was almost dark. Soldiers sorted through the bodies, looking for the few that were still alive and wounded, putting them on litters to take back to camp. I got myself up, scrabbled over Charlie's body as fast as I could, and ran in the direction of the camp. When I got back, nobody noticed me. Nobody talked to me. They were all in their own hellish world. I found my bedroll and went to the nearest tree, where I threw the blanket over my head, and hid myself from the monsters.

That is far more than you need to know. I could go on, but I would spare you any more details. I can tell that you feel what I feel when I describe the grisly horror. Doubtless it sounds like every man's story who was there. I can't say how or why I survived the fighting. I say now that it should never have been. When my time was done, I was grateful to leave that hell behind.

3

Trauma and Anguish, Death and After-Death

I was frozen in place as Joe told me his story, psychically hearing his voice speaking to me, a voice cracked with such traumatic awareness. I had no sentient knowledge of what happened to me as my body lay on the Reiki table. I was completely absorbed by Joe's consciousness and lost all connection with the reality that was my own. Although I couldn't see images of everything he described, every now and then a battlefield scene would appear in my mind's eye, scenes more horrific than Hollywood ever made them. Or a view of forest so thick the darkness lasted all day long as men trudged along a narrow path, walking totally detached, overcome with fatigue. These were real. These were Joe's memories. The fear and desperation infused my soul as he spoke with unbearable grief.

Then he was silent. The stillness overwhelmed me, sodden with his emotions. I was in pain, as he was, the epitome of mental anguish as I'd never known it. My whole being was saturated with his excruciating hurt. It seemed a long time, and still I couldn't move, couldn't escape from the scenes I witnessed and heard him describe. I thought we were done, and Joe relinquished all he carried in his soul since his death, all that he needed to tell to unburden his spirit and be freed of his torment.

He came back then, as abruptly as he left, and let me know he had more to tell me. I couldn't fathom what more misery burdened his troubled soul. I was wrong, completely wrong. This time I was going to experience it first-hand. There was something different about this next part of his story, though. As far as I knew at that point, it was still Joe who communicated with me, who sent me the message. But there seemed a subtle change in the tone, perhaps in the voice, as if the very essence and energy of the Spirit underwent a transformation.

I hadn't experienced anything like it in the past, but I had no time to consider what it might mean. Joe began the next scene before I could think about it.

I wanted, even expected, for all to be well. I couldn't rest easy. There was no peace for me. Whenever I shut my eyes, I saw men dead in pools of their own dark blood. I saw faces who looked up at me with dead eyes. I was afraid to sleep. The dreams were real. So real that I believed if ever I let myself go, I would physically be transported to the fields of blood and that unrelenting, merciless noise. And if I let myself go there, Death would take me. I wouldn't be able to evade it. I was twenty-six years old, afraid to die and afraid to live.

The doctor called it "soldier's heart," this reliving that became a living hell. I couldn't get into any routine. My help was needed on the farm. Lots of things had to be done – my father couldn't do it all himself. There were fences to be mended and fields to plow. I swear I tried to do all I could, to work the farm as it should be. I started early in the morning soon after daybreak, and kept at it as long as I could after dark. I thought that if I kept myself busy there would be no time for the pictures in my head that came from the dreams. But I was wrong. The more I worked, the more they plagued me. And always there was the thought that I should be the one in the pool of blood, not any of the others.

Finally, it was enough. I tried for two years to bring myself back, but I just couldn't stand the torment any more. The nagging thoughts and the pictures in my head never went away no matter how I tried. I never had a minute of peace or quiet. That's when I decided it was enough.

As Joe began to tell me this next part of his story, his spirit overtook my consciousness and I saw, heard, and felt everything as it happened to him, as if I inhabited his soul. I lived through every thought and every action with him, as if I were him.

I walked through the meadow down the road from our house about a half mile or so. I cut through our own fields and woods so nobody saw me on the road. The hound followed me, ran all about but never paid me any mind. I carried a long-barreled pistol with me. I knew this one wouldn't be missed from the barn. I only took four cartridges, hoped that was three more than I would need.

A line of trees marked the edge of the woods at the far end of the meadow, and that's where I was headed. I walked with steady and deliberate steps toward those trees, trying not to think much. I wanted to pretend I could enjoy the morning sun, the blue sky with floating white clouds, and the little bit of breeze. Bees hummed around the wild daisies and butter-and-eggs that grew all around me. I crushed a path through the tall grass as I went, releasing the fresh smell. A robin flew overhead and I heard a bob-o-link call off in the distance.

It was a beautiful summer morning, and that made it all right, I think. It felt proper that my last time on this earth should offer a moment of its beauty. I had enough of misery, and dark thoughts, and bloody memories. I needed light and wonder.

I reached the trees at the far end of the meadow. The dog ran off by now and I was alone. I lifted my leg high enough to straddle the stone wall that marked the property line. I walked some more, this time surrounded by trees and deadfall. Pricker bushes caught on my clothes, but I paid them no mind. I walked for a few hundred yards into the forest. It was darker than the meadow, but there was no question it was still daylight, not like those thick woods I dreamed where the sunlight never penetrated.

Finally, I stopped. This was far enough. I couldn't waste any more time if I wanted to get this done. I didn't dare let myself have time to think about it. I cocked open the hammer of the pistol, poured in the powder, and seated the ball. I lowered the hammer back down and cocked it all the way. Then I closed my eyes and shoved the barrel of the pistol between my lips and up against the roof of my mouth. I felt it poking me there, taunting me. My finger was poised on the trigger. I had every intention of blowing my brains and all the torturing visions right out through the back of my skull...

Wait!

Nooooo!

Please! I didn't want to die. I didn't want to stop living. I was strong. I could fight this. Hadn't I faced worse demons, living in the nightmare of my own mind for years? If I survived that hell for so long, surely I could figure out now how to survive longer. I couldn't let myself do this.

It was like I suddenly woke up and found myself in a position I knew I didn't want to be in. I started to shiver and sweat beaded up on my forehead. I let my lips go slack and slowly started to take the gun from my mouth. But as I lowered it to draw it out, the muscle in my index finger contracted and jerked back on the trigger...

Darkness. Total and complete stillness. A silent scream charged through my body. When the pistol went off, the barrel pointed straight at the back of my throat. At such close range, I knew the ball smashed its way through my spine at the neck and severed the spinal cord. I couldn't see or feel anything. I must have fallen to the ground and such a wound would kill me. But I wasn't dead, not quite yet, though I knew I was dying. I felt no pain but there was absolutely nothing I could do except know it was happening. My brain worked and I could still think, but it was so quiet and so calm. I didn't know how long it took for me to die but finally I faded away...

At this point, I regained my own consciousness. I was no longer living through Joe's memories. I was still on the Reiki table and I could tell my session was just about finished. I heard Pierre, who worked at my head, continuously clearing his throat and making an odd deep gurgling noise. Joe wasn't quite finished, though. He had a little more to tell me and a message for me.

And then I was me again, but in a different way. I knew I was dead, probably because I was aware of myself dying. I was out of my body now, but I wasn't sure what to do. I stayed and waited for somebody to come. I didn't tell anybody where I was gone off to this morning or what I planned to do. They weren't going to miss me for hours at least. So, I just stayed, waited.

I don't know how long it took, but it was a long, long time. Months or even years. Finally, a man I didn't know came along. It looked like he was out walking and happened to pass by the pile of rags and bones that once was me. It caught his attention and he prodded and picked at the pile a bit but seemed unsure what to make of it. He must have figured out finally it was a body. He put a marker next to my remains and left. After another while, more people came back with the man. I didn't recognize any of them. They gathered up what was left of me and took it away. I didn't follow them. There was no point. I just stayed where I was for another long time.

I think nobody ever knew what happened to me. Nobody ever realized who that pile of bones and rags might be. Then I found you and I knew I could tell you my story. I knew I could make you hear me and you would listen. I needed to have somebody know my story. Somebody had to know what happened to me and why.

I told him I understood, and that now his story was heard, he could move on to finally rest and find peace. He asked if he could stay with me. I told him no, he must allow his soul to take care of what it needed to do but maybe I would talk with him again some time. I felt his energy embrace me like a hug as he asked me for one last favor.

Will you make sure they all know? I want to be sure that they finally know what happened. Lady, will you tell my story?

I promised him I would and then he was gone.

The Reiki session was done and I slowly got up from the table. I asked my friends if they felt anything during the session. Pierre said he felt something in his throat, and it got stronger as he worked on my throat Chakra. He described it as a grating sensation or irritation, not really pain, in the back of his throat. The others said they felt a lot of strong energy release but couldn't describe anything else. I gave them a very brief and vague summary of the most important points of Joe's story, and let them know that his Spirit was gone from the room now. Then I just let it drop and we moved on to the next person's turn on the table. For them, it was another experience with the Spirit world through Reiki and certainly not uncommon. For me, it became much more.

4

Proving Joe Tripp Was a Real Person

How would I begin to figure out the details of Joe's story? After all this time, who was it that needed to know what happened to him?

I promised his Spirit I would do what I could to tell the story, and I intended to do that for his soul to find peace. He certainly deserved peace after the torment he went through during the war and after. I could write his story and publish it for all to read, but it had to be more than that. I needed to prove to those who might read it that there really was a Joe Tripp, and that his torment and anguish were real. I also needed to prove to Joe there was someone who cared about what happened to him. That someone, apparently, was me. I was the person he singled out in the hope that I would do what was necessary to end his suffering. I wasn't going to let him down.

In order to verify Joe existed and lived through these Civil War experiences, a few specific details about him and his life were essential. To start, I had to prove that Joe Tripp lived and that was his actual name. Although that seemed a bit basic and trivial, it really wasn't.

I often found Spirits got "confused" when reporting to the living what they perceived as facts. The transformation from living to other-worldly somehow failed to transfer memory properly and accurately. Usually all the pieces of the memories were there, but they got put together in different ways that didn't necessarily reflect our truth as it appeared in the realm of the living. The truth as we knew it in this world wasn't necessarily the reality as it existed beyond the grave and in other realms. Perception and interpretation sometimes took priority over what we saw as the actual sequence of remembered events.

In conjunction with determining the actuality of Joe Tripp as a once living person, I needed to focus in on a geographic location. Since Joe told me he traveled no farther from home than "the great city of

New Bedford," I was certain he was from the region around Westport, Massachusetts, the location where he came to me that day. Westport was only a few miles west of New Bedford, which was the whaling capital of the world during Joe's time.

My search had to encompass the area of southeastern New England. Bristol, Plymouth, and Barnstable Counties in Massachusetts as well as Newport County in Rhode Island. Tripp was, and still is, a fairly common surname in that entire geographic area. I too was a descendant of the Tripp family who settled the area in colonial times. My intuition told me that my own ancestral connection to the Tripps formed a bond with Joe. We shared bits of the same DNA. This link probably helped him find me and gave him hope that I would help him find peace. (See Part II – Section I)

To prove Joe was a real person, documentation was required that anchored him in a specific time and place. If he joined the army in 1861, he obviously should appear in the 1860 United States Census. After a thorough search of the census, I came up with four men, all named Joseph Tripp, who lived in the correct geographic area. My research led me through extensive analysis of supporting documentation for each of them in an effort to eliminate the individuals who could not be my Joe and determine which one he actually was. (See Part II, Section 2)

I thought for sure that one of those four men would be my Spirit, but it wasn't that easy. He was constantly on my mind as I tried to figure out how to solve this mystery. I asked the Universe for assistance, not knowing exactly what I wanted or expected for help.

One morning I woke up with a sharp jolt and my eyes popped open. I quickly closed them again and instantaneously received a vision. It was a Civil War soldier and I knew it was Joe. His face was young, shadowed with a hint of pale beard stubble. He wore a Union Army Civil War cap with military insignia on the band and on his collar. He looked straight ahead, with a pensive, almost emotionless, expression. The thought that I wished I could draw him flicked through my mind. Then his face morphed into that of an older man, perhaps in his forties, clean shaven with a full head of hair. This man looked straight ahead, emotionless. That face faded after several seconds.

I must have fallen asleep after the image was gone, because I once again woke with a start. This time I had a math problem in my head that didn't quite make sense. The problem went like this: If the Civil War soldier was forty-four years old and enlisted in 1865, he was born about 1820. In the story told me by Spirit Joe Tripp, he said he enlisted at age nineteen and was age twenty-six when he died. If nineteen was the year he was born and you add twenty-six you get forty-five, the age when he enlisted and fought in the war.

This certainly was a convoluted puzzle, but I never discounted any psychic messages as clues. Either the spirit tried to point me toward the one Joseph Tripp of Fairhaven who never gave his correct age, or there was a deeper meaning hidden behind the numbers. I had no way to know, but my intuition worked overtime and all I could think of was the memory of Joe Tripp seeming to have two different voices when he told me his story, one voice for the war and one for the suicide. I believed that the two faces of Joe Tripp in the image would prove significant and I remained open to all possibilities.

Three days later I received a psychic message that I should draw the image of the soldier I saw in my vision. I got a paper and pencil and started sketching right away. My hand felt like it was guided by some unseen energy force. The sketch was finished in only a few minutes. It wasn't a perfect reproduction of the face I saw but it was very close. I believed Spirit helped me draw the picture. I never sketched any of my visions before, but this encouraged me that I could do it again if I wanted to. I only needed to capture the image in my memory. I truly believed I now had a sketch of what my Joe Tripp looked like as a soldier, whether it might help me in my search for him or not.

Unfortunately, I had no similar memory of the image of the older man in the vision, and try as I might, I couldn't recall enough detail to sketch his face at all.

Spirit sketch of Civil War Soldier Joe Tripp

5

Skeletons, Cemeteries, and a Tour of Westport

I thoroughly researched and analyzed the information for all four men named Joseph Tripp who fought in the Civil War from Bristol County, Massachusetts. Every one of them had a sad tale to tell about their life. However, based on the facts I found, none of them was the Joe Tripp who told me the story of his accidental suicide.

I was convinced a ghost told me the story, as filled with emotion and anguish as the communication was. It wasn't just my overactive imagination at work. If Joe Tripp wasn't Joseph Tripp, then who was he? I carefully considered what my next steps should be. By no means, did I want to make the story fit the records. Otherwise, I would just accept one of the Joseph Tripps who fought as a Civil War soldier without the meticulous and thorough search to rule them all out.

During the time I researched all these Josephs, I often tried and hoped to make contact with Joe again, but I never connected with him. I wasn't sure whether, after the Reiki session, he felt assured enough of my promise that he was at peace and let his soul move on. Or perhaps it wasn't the proper time for me to receive any more communication from him and I would have to wait. Either way, that was all I could do, but I didn't intend to stop searching.

I reviewed my list of the nine Joseph Tripps who fought in the Civil War from any state, not just Massachusetts, and compiled basic information on all of them. I began a more in-depth search in the records from each state, and found specific information about the service record of each of those nine men and what happened to them during and after the war. I found enough information on each of them to rule each of them out. Not one of them could have been my Spirit Joe Tripp.

I started to feel a little doubtful about the whole story, I have to admit. With no particular direction, I started some random searches, in an effort to find clues to provide a focus. Online newspapers were my next option, to look for an article about a local missing soldier or remains found in the woods. During my first research session, I made a discovery that, while not definitive, was strong enough to revive my motivation. On a subscription newspaper site, I did a search in the New Bedford papers for "skeleton." There was one hit from the *Whaleman's Shipping List and Merchants' Transcript* of Tuesday morning, July 26, 1876:

"State Detective Oesting of this city, found part of a human skeleton in Westport Woods on the 18th inst. It had probably been there for twenty years and no one can account for it."

The same story was published in the *Springfield Republican* (Massachusetts) a few days earlier on July 20. I checked the other New Bedford and Massachusetts newspapers available online, but found nothing more. There was no follow up to the story through the rest of the year or into 1877.

Was this the lost skeleton of Joe Tripp, whoever he was, found years after the suicide? Was this Detective Oesting the man in the woods that Joe said found his remains? Why did Oesting think the remains were twenty years old and how reliable was that estimate? I needed to answer these questions.

I spent my early childhood in Westport, moving with my parents and sisters to another nearby town when I was eleven. A number of relatives still lived in the town, and we visited often when I was younger and occasionally in my adult years. I knew a lot about the geography of the town, and how to get around from place to place on the rural country roads. I never, however, heard of any location referred to as Westport Woods. This might have helped me narrow down the search, if I knew what part of town the Woods were in and which families lived near there.

My first thought was to look for some kind of investigation of the skeletal remains, particularly records from the medical examiner. After several calls, I reached the Director of the State Judicial Archives, a woman who was very knowledgeable and helpful. I learned from her that the state office of medical examiner was established in 1877. Prior to that date, a court inquest might be held only if the local officials deemed it necessary.

Because the date of the discovery of the skeleton in 1876 was so close, she thought it might have been included under the medical examiner's jurisdiction if the investigation wasn't concluded by the time the medical examiner was appointed. She cautioned me that if there was no evidence to go on, and therefore nothing to investigate, they would just bury the bones and be done with it.

She suggested the next step, as far as the skeleton was concerned, was to contact the Westport town cemetery department to determine if they had a record of burial for the unidentified bones. If that could be found, there might be enough information to check the archived records for a possible investigation. She hesitated to order these old records from deep within the archives vault without any specific evidence an investigation took place, with no specific date of inquiry. There could be hundreds of documents to sort through.

When I checked the website of the Westport Cemetery Department, I found there was a searchable online database. The website was an excellent resource and quite well done. There was a separate link to a list of veterans including the 107 Westport Civil War soldiers who were buried in the town. There was also a virtual veterans' cemetery for the ten Civil War veterans from town who were buried in various National Cemeteries under the U.S. Department of Veteran Affairs. The database contained grave and burial data for the three public cemeteries in town, as well as seventy-six of the private cemeteries, mostly burial grounds located on a family-owned property and, though not maintained by the town, were protected by Massachusetts law.

Using the database, I found the gravesite and burial information for Joseph H. Tripp, who died of typhoid fever in Virginia, buried with his parents in Beech Grove Cemetery. A search for just the surname Tripp produced 629 burial entries. Searching for unknown as a first or last name gave me a list of forty-five burials. There wasn't enough information about any of them to help me at that point.

I believed that better results were always achieved when you interacted with someone face to face. After several attempted phone calls and a message left on the answering machine, I still wasn't able to speak with anyone at the cemetery department. Since Westport was only a twenty minute drive, I decided to go there and try to find someone to talk with. My first stop was the cemetery office at Beech Grove in the Central Village section of town where I met one of the staff outside the office.

I told him I needed to check some burial records from 1876. He wanted to help but the records were recently transferred to a new computer system and he wasn't sure how to work with it yet. The "boss" could help me but he was on vacation and would be back on Monday. He asked me what it was about specifically. I explained my search for a Civil War soldier who accidentally committed suicide and showed him the article from the *Whaleman's Shipping List*. I told him I wanted information about the unidentified skeleton and hoped to find some connection with the soldier.

That immediately captured his attention, as he said "I never heard of that!" He stated he was really interested in that kind of thing, and that was something his boss would definitely be interested in helping me with too. He couldn't tell me where Westport Woods might be, though, and never heard of any such area referred to in town. He told me he would leave a note for his boss and that I should come back the following week.

When I left the cemetery, I decided on a whim to stop at the town hall and see if the Town Clerk's office might have any recorded burial for the skeleton. A pleasant woman in the office greeted me when I walked in. I gave her the same explanation as the worker at the cemetery, that I was searching for a Civil War soldier who accidentally committed suicide and was trying to match it with the brief article in the newspaper in 1876. When I showed her the article, her response was the same "I never heard of that!" She told me she would be happy to do some research for me in the records and let me know if she found anything. She couldn't let me look for myself in the old ledger books because they were too fragile, which I expected and appreciated. I asked her if she knew of anywhere in town that was known as Westport Woods, but she never heard of that either.

I drove out of town with a positive feeling that someone would come forth with information. Unfortunately, it didn't happen that way. I got an email from the woman at the town hall a few days later, reporting that she wasn't able to find anything related to my query. Over the next few days, I went through all the death records for Westport between 1866 and 1886, when I discovered that the actual pages were scanned and indexed in an online database. I found a few men for whom the cause of death was listed as "Suicide" or "Accidental Shooting," but none of them was an appropriate candidate for the skeleton in the woods or for my Spirit Joe Tripp. None of them, that I could find, were Civil War soldiers.

One record in particular caught my attention, though. On May 9, 1861 Edwin Slocum died in Westport and the cause of death was noted to be suicide by shooting. I searched for any more information and found an article in the *Boston Herald* newspaper published on May 14.

SUICIDE IN WESTPORT. Edwin Slocum, aged 21 years, son of Andrew and grandson of Humphrey A. Slocum, committed suicide in the entry of his father's house,

Westport, Saturday last, by shooting himself in the head. It
is thought that he was partially insane.

The circumstances of Slocum's suicide didn't match the
information I received from Joe Tripp. Edwin was in Westport and he
shot himself in the head, which was the same method, but it was in his
father's home, not in the woods as I saw in the vision. Certainly, the
body was found shortly after the event and didn't lie hidden for months
or years. Joseph H. Tripp of Westport must have known Edwin as they
were about the same age. This young man's death made an impression
on me, and I knew I would keep it in the back of my mind as I pursued
more research.

The following week, I met with the director of the Westport
Cemetery Department. He was very open to my search needs. He took
me to the area called the Potter's Field, the traditional designation for
the area of a cemetery where paupers or unknown/unidentified bodies
were buried. There were a couple of numbered markers there, but it was
mainly a grassy lot, fairly small in size compared to similar pauper lots
in other cemeteries I'd visited over the years.

I looked through the burial records and was disappointed to find
no dates for the Potter's Field burials, and only two recorded names.
One of those, George Mosher, was marked as a veteran, but there were
no dates. There was nothing there that could help me at all. I looked
through the rest of the records and jotted down a few names and dates
for other veterans that looked like they might be Civil War era for more
searching later on.

Although I didn't find an answer, I wasn't finished yet. The director
gave me a name and phone number for a woman in town who worked
on creating the online cemetery burial database. He thought if there
was anything unusual, she would know about it.

After I left the office, I drove over to the veterans' burial lots in the
center of the cemetery and took a quick look around, but didn't see

anything that caught my attention. Since I was alone in that spot away from the office, I decided to do a quick meditation to see if I could make contact with the ghost of Joe Tripp or whoever belonged to the skeleton found in Westport Woods.

It only took a few seconds to get a message. With my eyes closed, I saw the profile view of a man's head and shoulders, lying face up, and wearing a hood that shadowed most of his features. His head was turned slightly in my direction with the chin tilted forward and upwards. As I watched, he raised his eyes as if trying to look up and over his head. In my mind, I clearly heard him repeat over and over the phrase, "I am here. I am here. I am here." This lasted for about a minute before fading away. I asked him to direct me where I should go next, since I felt my visit to town wasn't yet finished. I immediately understood that I should drive down Drift Road, which wasn't far away, toward that section of town known as the Head of Westport. The contact ended and I started off on my next mission.

As I drove along, I remembered that the Westport Historical Society was at the end of Drift Road, at the Head. I visited there once many years previous. When I got to the Historical Society, there were cars in the parking area. I checked the sign out front and was surprised to see that it was only open two days a week, Monday and Wednesday, for a few hours each day. It just happened to be Wednesday so I knew it was exactly where I was supposed to go.

I met a very nice woman there, who really couldn't help me with my quest in any way, but asked if I had seen the book about the Westport Civil War soldiers. I thought she meant a booklet printed in 1983 that I purchased many years ago, but she went in back and brought out a brand new book which she said was recently published, titled *Biographies of Civil War Soldiers and Sailors of Westport, Massachusetts*. She didn't have any way for me to purchase one there, but told me of a local bookstore in town where I could get one, across the street from the cemetery where I was ten minutes earlier. She also gave me the contact information for one of the authors who she felt would be willing to talk with me.

Back I drove to the Village, to the bookstore across from the cemetery. I browsed around but didn't see the book, so I was disappointed since I felt it was supposed to help me or at least provide some clues to my mystery. As I walked toward the door to leave, I glanced down and spotted it on the bottom shelf in a corner. Relieved, I picked it up and noticed it was the only copy on the shelf. I didn't even bother to thumb through it, just hurried to the cash register to make sure I had it and was taking it home, as I believed this was the purpose toward which the spirit directed me.

A few days later, I spoke with the woman referred to me by the cemetery director. She told me she continued to maintain the online cemetery database and was intrigued when I told her my story about the skeleton in the woods. She agreed that the bones wouldn't be discarded even at that time period and would be buried in the Potter's Field if they were unidentified. As we spoke on the phone, we worked through the online database together.

After a few searches, we found a burial with both given and surname entered as "Unknown." The location of the burial was Beech Grove Cemetery, and the grave was noted as Section A1, Potter's Field, Grave 25. There was no other information. The date wasn't recorded. The date of death, date of birth, and age fields were filled in with zeroes, and the "Relatives" field stated "not specified." There was a comment attached, however, which read "Found in Letters and Journal of Westport Overseers 1848-1889. No dates given. States as Unknown taken from Schoolhouse Lot."

The woman didn't know where the Schoolhouse Lot might have been. She said the person who initiated the cemetery project found the Overseers' journals during her search for burial records and went through them to extract pertinent data. She thought she might be able to contact that person and would try to do that for me. This burial in

Potter's Field, with only the date range from the record book to give any perspective, plus the fact that no other information was recorded gave me hope this could be the grave of the skeleton in the woods.

I communicated by email with one of the authors and researchers of the Civil War soldiers book. He seemed quite interested in my two mysteries, but couldn't offer any additional information. After checking his records of Civil War soldiers for Westport and nearby towns, he found no soldier who died of a self-inflicted wound. He stated he found the story of the skeleton in the woods fascinating, but had nothing more to provide any clues. The one piece of information he gave me was that nearly all the burials in the paupers' graves in Potter's Field at Beach Grove Cemetery were individuals who died at the Westport Poor House from a known cause of death. So, what were the unusual circumstances related to the unknown, undated burial from the Schoolhouse Lot and how or why did it end up there?

I now had potentially four mysteries to solve.

Who was my Civil War soldier if he wasn't Joe Tripp?

Was Joe Tripp really the one with the accidental self-inflicted fatal wound?

Whose skeleton was found in the Westport Woods years after its death?

Who was the Unknown who was buried in the School House Lot and moved to the Potter's Field in Beech Grove Cemetery?

The questions of identity seemed to be piling up, and at this point I had no idea if there was any link between them, and if there was, what it could be. I only knew this was the direction that Joe Tripp was leading me, and there had to be a purpose behind it all.

6

Overseers of the Poor, The Schoolhouse Lot, and the Tripp-Davis Family Connection

I continued to search through records, trying to find any additional clue to the identity of my Joe Tripp. I read through every one of the 172 biographies of Westport's Civil War soldiers included in the book I bought. They were compelling reading, but I didn't find anyone that I thought could be Joe. There were no suicides, as the author advised. Neither did I find any soldier who disappeared without a trace.

It was at that point I discovered the Town of Westport website contained a treasure trove of digital, scanned copies of all kinds of town records dating back to the earliest days of the town, including pertinent early records of Dartmouth and New Bedford, Westport's parent towns. (Westport was set off and established in 1787.) It would take a while to browse through hundreds of pages of original records, but if I needed to do that I would.

My first goal was to look for the records that provided the information for Unknown posted on the cemetery database. Fortunately, the set of records titled "Letters and Journals of the Overseers" were scanned and posted. This was a collection of records from 1848 to 1887 for the town's Overseers of the Poor. (See Part 2, Section 3)

With a quick browse through the list of records, I managed to find the page in the Overseers' Journal that the information was taken from for the Unknown burial in the website database. The page contained a map of the paupers' gravesites with a list of seven names and corresponding grave numbers including the notation for "25 Unknown Taken from School House Lot." This was the same note that was recorded on the town cemetery website. There was nothing else to learn other than the mapped location of the grave.

After studying the information, I found that the burials occurred in successive order down two rows of thirty-six graves each. Based on the individuals buried before and after, I thought I could determine an approximate date of burial for Unknown's remains. I looked up the names in the town records to get the death dates. Based on these dates, the range for Unknown was between August 29, 1883 and September 29, 1884.

This time period over thirteen months wasn't out of line with the death of either my Spirit Joe Tripp or the removal of the skeleton found in the woods by Detective Oesting. If I could find a location for the School House Lot, I might be able to figure out a bit more about Unknown.

It took a lot of reading through a number of pages of the old town records, but I managed to find some relevant information. I reviewed a ledger book of permits granted by the Westport Selectmen to disinter bodies from one burial place so they could be buried in another. Most often these were requests made by family members or land owners to move remains from a small family plot located on private property, to another location for interment, frequently to a family plot in a larger public cemetery. There were also permits for the town Undertaker to remove a corpse from a residence for burial in a cemetery. All of these requests had to be granted through the town Selectmen.

On October 21, 1884, the following permit was approved:

"Permit granted Charles Fisher to disinter the remains of George W. Davis, Hannah Davis and Sarah G. Davis in a burial ground near School House No. 7, and remove the same to South Cemetery in N. Bedford for interment ~ Also the remains of a person unknown and remove the same to

Beech Grove Cemetery in Westport for interment in the Potter's Field.

G. E. Brownell} Selectmen of Westport"

This clearly was the permit to remove the remains of my Unknown for reburial. The date of the permit was twenty-three days later than I estimated, so either they left an open grave site for some unknown reason and buried two other bodies around it, or the body was moved before the actual permit was granted. Either way, I now was certain of a very narrow time span when Unknown was moved from the burial lot near School House No. 7, though I still didn't know where that burial lot or School House was located.

Reading through the Town Meeting records I found that the school districts were laid out in 1802, but I couldn't find the report or minutes of that meeting. In the 1827 Town Report, there was a list of the men who were appointed to head the "Prudential Committee" for each of the nineteen school districts of the time. The prudential officer for District No. 7 was William T. Davis.

By looking closely at a number of maps posted on the Westport Historical Documents website, I found a map dated 1858 which identified each school by number. School House No. 7 was located on what is now Cornell Road near the intersection with Main Road in the area that included the upper reaches of the West Branch of the Westport River (also known as the Acoaxet River). According to historical maps from the period of the 1830s to the 1850s, it was sparsely settled with large areas of wooded undeveloped land. There were several Tripp families that lived in the area listed on these maps.

Using census records, I realized that the burial ground near the school house was probably on the family homestead of one particular Davis family, originally Benjamin Davis and later his son George Washington Davis. By 1810, there were Tripp families living nearby.

I searched through the town land and probate records to gather information on Benjamin and his son. (See Part 2, Section 4)

For some reason, after finding the probate records for Benjamin, I felt a strong pull to check the Westport Town records again. Intuition or premonition, I wouldn't ignore the psychic directives. Not exactly sure what I was supposed to be looking for, I started with tax records and moved on to Town Accounts which contained a number of entries paid to both Benjamin and William Davis, who ran a store on their homestead. William served a term as Town Selectman.

When I checked the records on the town cemetery website, I found there was a William Davis Burial Ground on Cornell Road, not far from the corner with Main Road, that abutted the property where School House No. 7 was located. This was right next to the area I believed was the property of Benjamin and George W. Davis where Unknown was originally buried. According to the town's description, the William Davis Burial Ground contained nine marked gravestones and no unmarked stones. Of these graves, I knew three others besides the elder William. William Thomas Davis was the prudential officer for School District No. 7, and his parents, Philip and Sarah Davis, who I believed were my fifth great-grandparents.

I began to wonder where all this was going to lead. There wasn't only a Tripp familial connection in my own family tree, an ancestry probably shared with Joe Tripp. I was now finding a Davis familial connection shared with Unknown. From the gravestone inscription, I had a birth and death date for William Davis, Esquire. I decided to check for probate records for him. This is when the reason for this psychic premonition became perfectly clear to me.

William Davis's will clearly outlined family relationships and identified an error in my own family research. For many years, I claimed the wrong ancestor and their line back several generations, although both lines traced back to the same early colonial ancestor. I never would have questioned this or discovered the truth if I hadn't researched the Spirit of Joe Tripp, Unknown from the Davis family burial ground, and the Skeleton in the woods. I was more convinced than ever there was a familial blood connection between me and these Spirits, and they were guiding me along this path.

I researched the antecedents of this Davis family, and, the more I researched the Davis family, the more connections I found to the Tripp family as close neighbors with family inter-marriages. What I didn't find, though, was what I was really looking for. There was no reference, however slight, to the burial of the skeletal remains that were found by Detective Oesting in 1876.

I decided to check at the Westport Library and see if anything more was available there than online. I was pleased to discover that the library had a designated room housing a large collection of town and local history documents and references. It was nice to reaffirm that Westport considered the efforts to preserve its history of significant value.

My first priority was to look through the available maps for any that weren't scanned and posted to the website. All the maps were labeled and indexed, so it was easy to find a few that I hadn't previously reviewed. First and foremost, these maps confirmed that the Davis and Tripp families were neighbors in the Acoaxet area. It was also very useful to be able to put the lots of land belonging to the various residents of the area in perspective graphically, being able to see whose lands abutted and who the immediate neighbors were.

One map was particularly helpful, and though it wasn't dated, the caption written along the bottom stated "Shows Early Landowners." The hand-drawn map outlined the boundaries of each lot and had the owner's name hand-printed inside the property lines. Benjamin Davis's name was printed in two adjacent lots. All around these lots were familiar names of Ebenezer Tripp, James Tripp, Joseph Tripp, Abial Tripp, Peleg Tripp, John Tripp. I saw all these names in the Survey Books when the land was being laid out to the Dartmouth Proprietors in 1713 and 1714, and in other records as well. I certainly had enough validation that the ancestral family of the Spirit Joe Tripp probably lived here, alongside the Davis family.

I looked at a number of other documents that day at the library, which helped me glean a better understanding of the area and the successive generations of these families that occupied their homesteads. I found a copy of applications made to the Massachusetts Historical Commission in October 1988 for the purpose of placing two of the Davis houses on the state Historical Register. Both applications had photographs of the houses as they stood at that time. One of these two houses, with a current address at the corner of Cornell Road and Main Road, was described as a store with a residence and was on a private lane off a rural road surrounded by woods and fields. The application for the other Davis house gave an address on Cornell Road, next door to the first, stating it was at the end of a laneway seven-tenths of a mile long off a rural road in fields and woods.

There was still nothing to tell me who Unknown was, and whether he was connected to these Tripp or Davis families.

7

Archives, Archives Everywhere, But Not a Shred of Proof

As I worked on research of the Davis family and their connection to Unknown, I tried to follow up other leads that could help me identify Skeleton. I already determined that the state Medical Examiners weren't appointed until a year after Detective Oesting found the remains in the woods, so there was no documentation there. There might have been other official police documents, however, and that was my next avenue to explore.

I called my cousin Bill who, though now retired, was a police officer and later the police chief in Westport for many years. He lived in the town all his life and knew most of the people and families, as well as a substantial amount of the history and historical gossip. I had a few questions for Bill, and he was happy to help. First of all, he said he never heard of any place in town being specifically called Westport Woods. I explained about Detective Oesting and the Skeleton. Bill didn't think Westport had an actual police department back in the 1870s, and if anything, might have had only a constable. During his tenure at the police department, he never saw any records that old. The oldest he recalled went back only to the 1920s or 1930s, but no earlier than that.

Bill did have a couple of suggestions, though. His first thought was to check with the town library to review their collection of old maps and other historical documents, which I had already done. Then he suggested I contact the owner and director of the Potter Funeral Home in town. Potter was another distant relative, and I'd known him since I was a child, since all our relatives were always buried from there. Bill said the original funeral service was called Potter and Hicks, and was in at least two other locations in town before its present one. The business was around for many decades, though he wasn't sure how far back, and he knew they still had most of their old burial records stored away.

Bill gave me another name of a man, called "Westie," who lived in town and was quite old. Bill said Westie's father worked for the town but the family was involved with the Potter and Hicks funeral business, so he might know something about the situation or have suggestions about where else to look.

I called Potter's Funeral Home and spoke with a young woman who asked that I send her an email with the information I was looking for. There were some records that were dated before 1900, but she wasn't sure how far back they went. I got her response back very quickly after I sent her the information. Unfortunately, the Potter Funeral Home was established in 1892 and there were no records before that date. She told me she would make some inquiries and would let me know if she found any other possible information.

I contacted Westie, the man that my cousin Bill referred me to, who was proud to tell me he was one of the oldest citizens in Westport. He also let me know he served as the head of the cemetery department in town for many years. He was interested in my story and provided some background historical information for me, but wasn't able to shed any additional light on my mysteries. He never heard anything about Skeleton or the burial of Unknown.

While all this was going on, I followed up on what I thought might be another possible source for documents related to Skeleton. The Massachusetts State Police maintained a museum and learning center in Grafton, and their website indicated they were the repository for the state police records archives. The Massachusetts State Police was established in 1865, so they were still a fledgling organization when Detective Oesting found the Skeleton.

I made contact with Mr. Guilmette who was on the Board of Directors of the museum and a historian himself. I explained what I was researching and what I was hoping to find. Mr. Guilmette advised that he researched some of the earliest state policemen for his own book and Charles Oesting was one of them. He was already aware of the skeleton found by the detective. He offered to send me a biographical piece about Oesting and some contemporary newspaper articles about investigations and arrests Oesting was involved in. He was sorry to say, however, that there were no documents, reports, or logs left behind by Oesting or any of the other early detectives, about any of their investigations, including the skeleton in Westport.

Mr. Guilmette searched for these records for five years and to date hadn't found any. There were very few records in the state archives and almost no police reports from the period survived. He doubted there was any Court involvement unless some type of court action was needed following an investigation. He thought there might have been a coroner's inquest to attempt to determine the identity of the remains and cause of death, and this might have been reported in the local newspapers at the time. It was also possible that a local official, selectmen, or constable would be called to the scene so town hall journals or records from the period might contain a reference.

The New Bedford Library housed a large collection of historical newspapers on microfilm, so I decided to search for more references to Skeleton or to Detective Oesting himself. Unfortunately, only a few years of one paper were indexed. I did review that index first, but there was no mention of anything related to Skeleton. That meant sitting at the microfilm reader and scanning and reading page after page of issue after issue of newspapers. Although New Bedford boasted several throughout its history, I started with one that was pretty popular and provided general news for a number of years. This was the New Bedford *Republican Standard Weekly*. Knowing that the skeleton was discovered just before July 20, 1876, I thought I would start with June that year. I scanned, browsed, and read every page of every issue of the paper from June 8 through December 28, but there wasn't one article or reference to the discovery of the skeleton in the Westport woods. After spending several hours at this task, I questioned if this was the most productive use of my time.

Next, I contacted the Bristol County Sheriff's Office in hope there might be some historical archives I could access and find a reference to the Sheriff being consulted by Detective Oesting. I was told that all the historical records from the sheriff's office were transferred to the Massachusetts State Archives in Boston and they could be accessed there. On the Archives' website, I found the catalog of the Sheriff's records. Disappointed once again, I learned that almost all these surviving records were related to the administration of the old Bristol County jails, and although they did contain personal information about inmates and other miscellaneous reports, there was no log or documentation related to the activities of the Sheriff himself.

I was disappointed and frustrated. This was a state that prided itself on its rich history, going back 400 years. There were archives everywhere in Massachusetts for everything you could think of and serious efforts to preserve historical documents and artifacts were a first consideration in all projects. Yet, the few pieces of information I needed to help me solve these mysteries were nowhere to be found.

8
Finding the Skeleton with Detective Oesting

I decided to use the spiritual Akashic Records to try and receive insight. The Akashic Records could be thought of as the Great Library of the Universe containing the virtual Book of Life for every soul that ever lived, and a spiritual record of the entire history of all the past lives and future lives for each and every soul since Creation. They were an ethereal record of all human events, thoughts, words, emotions, and intent ever to have occurred in the past, present, or future. An Akashic Records Practitioner could enter the etheric plane where the records were stored and access the story of any soul at any given time and in any given life. I received my certification as a Practitioner in 2016 after a year's study.

I believed I might be able to use the knowledge of the Akashic Records to help me sort out some of the details of my three mystery Spirits. One of the basic tenets for using the Akasha, though, was that a practitioner wasn't allowed to access records of another individual without their consent. I felt Joe Tripp gave me his permission when he requested me to validate the circumstances of his death and to communicate that information to put his soul to rest. I believed the spirit that I called Unknown, whose remains were removed from the Davis land, acknowledged me and gave me permission to prove his story on the day he called out to me when I was meditating at Beech Grove Cemetery. Although I never interacted specifically with the spirit of Skeleton in the woods or been given consent to access his Akashic Record, I could certainly try to establish his relationship with the other two Spirits as I viewed their records. It was worth a try to see what I might come up with.

I entered the realm of the Akasha through meditation where I received visions and images to tell a story, like a dream or a video in my mind's eye. I was brought to a rural scene, with a man riding a horse along a hard-packed dirt road. The sun shone over trees that lined the road ahead and was high in the east, indicating late morning. He traveled south and I immediately knew that the man was State Detective Charles Oesting. In my vision I followed along behind him, trailing his progress. He wore a bowler hat, a long loose top coat, and boots. The horse was brown and rather non-descript, but looked well cared for.

The detective rode along on this country road until he came to an intersection with a dirt-packed road veering off to the right. A small building ahead on the left side near the corner, looked to be the school house. He slowed and hesitated at the dirt road as if making up his mind which way to go, but started up again and turned right onto the intersecting road. After a quarter mile, he stopped the horse, scanned the area, and dismounted. He led the horse to the north side of the road and tethered it to a low tree limb nearby on the edge of a large meadow.

Oesting studied the landscape ahead of him for a minute and then started walking diagonally across the field toward a stand of trees. I understood that he was there that day to look for a still hidden in the woods. After about five minutes, he reached the trees. It wasn't thick, but there was a lot of low-growing brush and deadfall. He continued on the same path into the woods for about another hundred feet and then turned due west, parallel to the tree line and at ninety degrees from the road, picking his way through piles of fallen leaves and deadfall, around saplings and brush.

I continued along behind him, and although I wasn't physically there, I saw him and everything he saw. He carried a long stout stick and poked in piles of brush, into stumps, and under stones, continuously surveying the area around and ahead of him. After a while, we came to the top of a very large boulder protruding from the ground. It was about two and a half feet high with a diameter of about four feet. There was a pile of leaves and twigs on one side of the rock, and something fluttered slightly at the side of the pile. Detective Oesting noticed it too and walked directly over. It was a small strip of ragged cloth stuck on a twig. He walked over and pulled it from the pile to examine it. The fabric was faded and worn but looked like it once had a colored pattern.

He put the rag in his pocket and kicked around the edges of the pile. Finding nothing more, he poked around with his stick while kicking at the leaves. His foot struck a solid object and he bent over to brush the leaves aside with his hand. He grabbed at something to retrieve it and held up a small bone. He looked at it closely and then put it in his pocket along with the rag.

He spotted a stick with a few stems and dead leaves still attached to the end, and used it like a broom to sweep the area. As he carefully cleared away the pile, he uncovered a number of additional bones forming part of a skeleton, most of the rib cage, spine, and both arms. The bottom half of one leg was gone and the other leg was separated from the hip. Several bones were missing, but there was no doubt it was a human skeleton. A few strips of ragged cloth were stuck to the bones. The skull was detached from the top of the spine and lay several inches away. He crouched over and studied the skeleton without disturbing it. He then took his sweeping stick and cleared the area around the bones.

A few feet away, he found something else which he picked up gingerly and held in front of his face to examine more closely. It looked like an old pistol grip with part of a barrel rusted and broken away. He took the small bone from his pocket and placed it back with the others. He placed the pistol carefully down on the ground and proceeded to sweep the leaves and brush back over the skeleton to cover it up. He took a handkerchief from his pocket and tied it to his poking stick, which he then drove into the ground as a marker. Oesting seemed excited and agitated but he carried out these tasks in a deliberate and concentrated manner.

He picked up the rusted pistol, put that in his pocket and turned to get his bearings. He strode in a straight line toward the road and then along the shoulder. When he reached his horse, he took a cloth from the saddle bag and carefully wrapped it around the pistol before placing it into the bag. He mounted his horse and turned back toward the corner where the school building was. There was a farm house across the road from the school, and Oesting rode into the yard. He dismounted and approached a man who was working near a shed to the side of the yard. I saw the detective speak to the man for a few minutes, and then get on his horse and ride off again. The vision ended there.

This session in the Akashic Records, while not giving me direct or specific answers to my questions, offered me some thought-provoking information. I was aware that my own thoughts or experiences might influence the visions I saw while meditating, but I never completely discounted any of the messages. While the memory of the vision was fresh in my mind, I wrote notes about what I saw.

The vision indicated to me that the skeleton Detective Oesting found was in some woods near a meadow, consistent with Joe Tripp's story. It was off a main road at an intersection with a small building like a school house on the corner, which would match the location of School House No. 7 and the location of the Davis family burial ground where Unknown was originally buried. Although I try never to make assumptions from the messages and communication I receive, this vision from the Akashic Records seemed to imply at least a connection of some kind for my three mystery Spirits.

9

A Visit to Acoaxet

On December 7, 2018, I drove to Westport. It was a beautiful late fall afternoon, with a hint of winter in the air. The sun shone in a near cloudless sky, the wind was calm, and the temperature was a mild forty-two degrees. I was on a mission. I drove past the center of town, by Beech Grove cemetery and continued down Main Road. Within a few minutes, I came to the intersection with Cornell Road. I drove by, staying on Main Road. I wanted to see what the area looked like on all sides. Obviously, it was more built up now than it was in my vision of Detective Oesting, even far more than I remembered from my childhood rides down this same road. But there were still many fields and stands of trees and I had a pleasant sense of familiarity.

I turned the car around and headed back toward Cornell Road. I had the addresses of the Davis houses, and, as soon as I turned the corner, I saw them on the right. The first one closest to Main Road was set back with a long drive and was up on a slight rise. There was a lot of growth and trees between the house and road, but the branches were mostly bare and I had a good view of the house. I didn't want to intrude on anyone's privacy or seem suspicious, so I just drove slowly by. The second Davis house was next door but my view of it was more obstructed by overgrown brush and trees. At least I knew both houses were still there, where I expected them to be.

Just a few feet down the road, on the opposite side, was the entrance to a narrow private road. I knew from my research that this was the road that led to the William Davis property where the private Davis family burial ground was located. William Davis, who owned the store with his brother Benjamin, and his family were buried there. There was a sign warning that this was private property and not a public way.

I drove along the road slowly. There was no other traffic and I was able to take my time. In less than a mile, I came to an area of fields and woods with no houses in my line of sight. My intuition told me it was the right spot, so I turned around and pulled over next to some woods on the south side of the road. I got out and immediately felt the energy all around me. I closed my eyes and took in deep breaths of the clean crisp air, feeling my spirit align with that of the place. There was a low stone wall that ran between the road and the deep stand of trees directly in front of me.

I crossed the road to the other side where another stone wall separated the road from more trees, though the woods seemed thicker here. The wall was obviously very old with a few stones tumbled onto the ground on either side, though mostly intact, and went on for quite a distance in both directions. At this spot, there was a strip of clear ground on the other side of the wall, but not far from there the trees took over.

There were a few evergreens, but most were birch, oak, and maple. The limbs were bare and I could see a distance into the forest. Since it was mid-afternoon, the sun was halfway to the horizon in the west, but its rays blazed through the branches on my left, casting long crooked shadows across the underbrush and the ground. I brought my camera with me and took several photos of the entire area from all angles.

I turned to my left and walked toward a break in the trees about fifty yards ahead. I took more pictures of the woods as I walked along. At the clearing where the trees ended, a large field opened up in front of me. A small gully overgrown with bushes and brambles served as a barrier along the road. The field was bordered by trees on the other three sides. I guessed the field was about an acre, though I'm not a good judge of those kinds of measurements and it was an irregular shape, narrow at the east end near where I was standing and deep and wide on the west side. The ground was muddy. A few puddles of standing water filled in ruts made by tractor tires. There were rows of yellowed and dried stubble from whatever grew there earlier in the year. I imagined it as it might have looked in the summer sunshine, green and lush with tall grass and wild meadow flowers.

This was the place. I knew it with my whole being. As I looked across the field toward the west, I pictured in my mind's eye the young man as he waded through the tall meadow grass on a sunny summer morning, soaking in the sights and sounds and smells for what he intended was the last time. I felt the sadness in him as he plodded his way to the trees that became his final resting place. It was private property now, and I had no right to trespass, or any desire to walk that long distance to the trees. I knew there was nothing left to find there. After taking a few more photos, I headed back to the car.

I drove to the intersection where Cornell Road met Main Road, where the small burial lot once stood next to the old school. The building was gone now too. The whole area was still rural enough, however, for me to recognize that this was exactly the place I saw in the Akashic Records vision of Detective Oesting.

There was nothing left here but the emotional energy infused deep within the place and the memory of that fateful day when a distressed young man took his own life and eventually became the Skeleton in the woods. I knew in my heart and in my soul that the story of the accidental suicide was true, even though I couldn't prove it belonged to the Spirit Joe Tripp.

Top photo is of the woods along Cornell Road not far past the old Davis homestead property. The bottom photo is the field just beyond that point where I believe the remains of Skeleton was found among the trees in the woods beyond the back perimeter of the field. (Photos taken by author.)

10

Revelations

By now, anyone who read this would have said, "What's the point? Just admit that you can't prove this ghost story. Just admit there was no ghost and the whole story was in your imagination."

There was no way to articulate the feeling of certitude, of unequivocal knowing, that I felt as the Spirit of Joe Tripp related his story to me. No explanation would make anyone understand how profound and unconditional this knowledge was. I couldn't articulate in words what it was like to relive someone else's traumatic life experience, watching events unfold through their eyes, feeling the same intense emotions that person felt as I experienced the same physical sensations at the same time they did.

I needed to sort this all out. As I continued to search, I believed that eventually all these mysterious connections would come together. The puzzle was always there for me. Was Unknown actually the Skeleton in the woods, and was Skeleton the remains of the accidental suicide victim? Were either of them Joe Tripp or were they someone else?

I totally and completely believed with all my heart and being that the story was true and I would solve the mystery. I was the person all of them chose, whether by design or serendipity. These questions were on my mind all the time, as I researched in the records or went about my daily routine. The story Joe Tripp told me affected me far more than any other I ever received from a spirit. I understood that one day I would write Joe's story and send it out into the world, so those who needed to know would be able to find it, as he asked of me.

Even as I continued my research, I began to write. I went back in my journal and reviewed my notes of the Reiki session when the Spirit of Joe Tripp first contacted me. I drafted his story as he told it to me that night, editing it only enough for the narrative to flow naturally.

As I wrote, I came to that break in the message, the interlude between his war-time experiences and his accidental suicide. Even in my notes at the time, I wrote of a noticeable difference in the tone of the story between the two, as if there were two narrators. I read about my dream-image, recalling the young face of the soldier that transformed into an older man's face as I watched, as if they were two different individuals. I wrote about my experience at the cemetery in Westport, and I remembered the vision of the shrouded body calling out to let me know he was there. The body that was Unknown called to me from his grave in the Potter's Field, while I knew a soldier Joseph H. Tripp was buried in the family plot with his parents elsewhere in the cemetery.

Suddenly, I had a blast of enlightenment and it all became crystal clear. Finally, I understood. I was thunderstruck. And I knew without any doubt. Two distinct individuals were tangled up in Joe Tripp's story. The residual energy of these two became intertwined, inextricably fused into one memory made from two traumatic events. I never dealt with any similar circumstance involving Spirits before, but that didn't mean it couldn't happen. I knew that powerful stress-induced emotion could trigger all sorts of manifestations in the physical world, so why not in the spiritual realm as well.

It suddenly made so much more sense to me. There were two spirits, one who lived through the horrors of battle and the other who ultimately experienced death by his own hand. My psychic sense told me that the one absorbed all the emotion-laden, tortured memories of the other and made them his own, creating that hell of dreams and visions which pursued and propelled him toward his fatal accident. This must have forced the two tormented souls to become fused, a dual Spirit with one set of memories.

As I pondered over this revelation, I speculated about what circumstances had to exist for two Spirits to coalesce into one voice with a single purpose. An internet search of religious tenets and literature throughout history provided a multitude of examples of two or more Spirits being merged in a single physical body. More currently there have been scientific studies of rare but medically verified cases of a single individual having two separate DNA strands, particularly where two separately fertilized eggs fused and became one embryo. If these examples can happen in the physical world, it surely was possible for similar situations to occur in the spiritual realm as well. Physical or spiritual, all activity and every being is dependent on energy and that energy is eternal.

First, in order for this fusion to take place, it seemed logical there needed to be some proximity in time and in location. I had a definite location for Skeleton and Unknown, both in Westport, where Joseph Tripp lived. I knew Unknown's exact location before being re-interred in Beech Grove Cemetery was in the Acoaxet area in a grave on private property that belonged to the Davis family going back to the original Benjamin Davis.

For Skeleton, I only knew a generic designation of "Westport Woods" where his remains were discovered. Although I suspected that Skeleton and Unknown were the same individual, I had no proof. As much as I personally had faith in the visions and messages I received that Skeleton was found in the woods near the Davis property on Cornell Road, there was nothing I could show to support that premise. It was true, however, that the remains of Skeleton found in the woods in 1876 by law had to be buried and not discarded because they were human remains. Since there was no official record of an original burial in one of the public cemeteries in town, it stands to reason that Skeleton was buried in a private lot on private property.

I also had Joe Tripp who was a resident of Westport and a soldier in the Civil War. Everything I discovered about Joseph H. Tripp, the Civil War soldier from Westport, matched the information the Spirit Joe Tripp provided me in his psychic story, except that he hadn't died of suicide. This new revelation brought me to believe that he was one of these distinct Spirits whose residual energy became fused.

He was the Civil War soldier who underwent such harrowing and horrifying experiences on and off the battlefield. He watched his two friends die, one shot and killed while the other suffered from the terrible disease which eventually brought about his own death. Joe was seventeen years old, three months shy of his eighteenth birthday, when he went off to war, and hadn't yet reached his nineteenth birthday when he died nine months later, alone and suffering in an Army field hospital far from home and family.

Joseph H. Tripp, at the time of his enlistment, lived in Westport with his parents Preserved and Lydia Tripp. His father was born in Westport, and based on the early census records from 1790 to 1840, his grandfather Joseph Tripp was from the Acoaxet area as were the generations before him back to the soldier's fourth great-grandfather James Tripp, one of the original proprietors of the area when it was still a part of Dartmouth in the late seventeenth and early eighteenth centuries. James Tripp was a close neighbor of the earliest Benjamin Davis, as shown on the historical maps.

This geography tied them all together in a common location. If there was more than one spirit, I felt confident I could identify Joseph H. Tripp of Westport as the Spirit Joe Tripp who made contact with me during the Reiki session.

As for proximity in time, I knew precisely the dates of Joe Tripp's military service and his death during that service. He enlisted on September 2, 1861 and died of Typhoid Fever on June 18, 1862 near the battlefield in Virginia. According to the records of Beech Grove Cemetery in Westport, his body was interred in the grave with his parents.

Unknown's body was interred at that same cemetery, moved there from his original grave on the Davis property in Acoaxet around September or October 1884. Obviously, Unknown died some time before then, and either his identity was unknown at the time of death or it was lost from memory.

Skeleton was found in the woods somewhere in Westport on July 1876 and State Detective Oesting estimated at the time of discovery that the body had been there about twenty years, though there is no remaining evidence of how or why he reached that conclusion. The Spirit who related the story of his accidental suicide said that he suffered with the dreams for two years, which could indicate that he died two years after the soldier.

Based on these postulated dates, these three individuals died within a span of no more than twenty years. I believe it was much closer than that. I found no evidence to eliminate the theory they all died within a couple of years of each other.

Obviously, Joe Tripp spent an arduous nine months as a soldier who saw action on several occasions, and most likely suffered a painful death from Typhoid Fever. I never found any clue to Skeleton's cause of death, but the fact that the remains were found in the woods near a settled area lends credence to the likelihood that he/she hadn't died of natural causes or events. Since Unknown's identity was never discovered, the circumstances of his/her death were still to be determined, though his connection to the Davis family and through them to the Tripp family was indisputable.

I was convinced the Joe Tripp who spoke to me during the Reiki session was the boy soldier from Westport. He fit the description and circumstances that the Spirit gave me. Originally thinking that Joe Tripp was the suicide, I tried to identify a man of that name who was a Civil War soldier and also a suicide. There was none. I found a few other men in Westport whose cause of death was noted as suicide by shooting in the head, but their bodies were found and identified soon after. This wasn't the case with the Spirit who told me his story.

But, as I have come to understand, Joseph Tripp wasn't the young man who suffered from severe depression, who agonized through tortured dreams that haunted his every waking moment, whose emotional status was so fragile that he thought the only escape was suicide. Who was that young man? I desperately tried to identify him, and finally concluded that he was an unknown body buried in a pauper's grave.

I was convinced since the day I read the article of Detective Oesting finding the skeleton in the woods that those remains belonged to that sad young man who shot himself. I believe that after the skeleton was found and couldn't be identified, a decision was made for the remains to be interred in a nearby burial lot, a location that was close to the scene of his discovery and assumed to be close to his home. This scenario made sense to me, since burial of the remains was required by law and they couldn't be disposed of in some other manner. Without contemporary documentation, there was no way to dispute or to prove this theory.

The memory of what I found about Edwin Slocum came back to me. He was described as partially insane. I wasn't completely sure what that phrase meant in 1861, but I was convinced that he suffered his own torment and horror. I did know, however, that he committed suicide by shooting himself through the head according to the newspaper account. Edwin's death was in May 1861, four months before Joseph Tripp enlisted in the Army. Edwin was distantly related to the Tripp and Davis families, and his ancestral lines included several families who lived in or near the same area of south Westport and Dartmouth. However, Edwin shot himself in the entry of his father's home, and his body was found within a short time after he died. He wasn't the Skeleton in the woods. He was buried in Beech Grove Cemetery, in the lot with his parents, so he wasn't Unknown buried in the Potter's Field. Yet, I could only speculate that perhaps his tortured Spirit might have lent some of the intense energy of his suicide to the fusion of these unfortunate souls.

11

A Last Visit

In June 2019, after I finished writing Joe's story, I made one more visit to Beech Grove Cemetery. I wanted to visit the grave of the soldier Joseph H. Tripp, which I hadn't done on my previous visit. I knew the location of the grave site and found it without a problem. Joe was in his own grave, buried in the lot with his parents, Preserved and Lydia, and his grandparents, Joseph and Anna Tripp. Other Tripp lots, belonging to other relatives, were all around that one.

I was surprised to see that there was no flag and no Civil War medallion beside Joe's gravestone, though the stone was engraved with the legend that he was a member of the 22nd Regiment Mass. Volunteers. His stone was in the back of the lot, the only gravestone in that row. I stood silently as I looked at all the stones and offered my respects. I touched the top of Joe's gravestone and felt nothing but peace and calm. There was no residual energy connected to his grave. I didn't receive any psychic message, but I sensed that Joe's spirit was at rest. I believed I helped him find that peace.

From where I stood at Joe's grave, I could see the Potter's Field ahead of me, just a short distance away. I moved toward the path that separated the plots. I felt no need to go any closer. I knew I wouldn't get any communication from Unknown either. I believed that Unknown wouldn't be able to send me a message without the boost of Joe's spirit energy. My psychic sense told me that the two Spirits were able to separate, no longer sharing the same emotional burden.

Joe Tripp's gravestone (top) and the view of the Tripp family lot (bottom) with Joe's grave in the back row and in the front row his parents and grandparents. (Photos taken by author, 25 June 2019.)

The view of the Potter's Field burial lot at Beech Grove Cemetery with the arrow showing the approximate location of the burial of Unknown who was removed there from the Davis family private cemetery near School House No. 7 on Cornell Road. (Photo taken by author, 25 June 2019.)

I was satisfied that I gave closure and peace to Joe Tripp. He died an excruciating death following the hellacious experience of war. He was only a teenager, a boy alone without the comfort of his family. He watched his friends die around him, and knew his own death approached. He wanted his story to be told so others would know he was a brave soldier, even as the terror and pain overtook him, and his sacrifice wouldn't be forgotten.

I wasn't able to give that same closure to the troubled soul who accidentally took his own life. Or at least not fully. While I didn't discover his identity, I was able to tell his story as he asked of me. There are those he felt needed to know what happened to him, but not knowing his name, I couldn't do that for him.

There are also those he wanted to know his story for another reason. He wanted them to know that in the end he chose to fight for his life, and, even though he unwillingly lost that battle, he had decided his life was worth fighting for. Together we told that message to all who needed to hear it.

Although this is the end of the story, it isn't the end of my efforts to identify the spirit who killed himself. It isn't the end of my search for the identities of Unknown and Skeleton, whether they are the same or separate individuals. I will continue to search at every opportunity and in every new record that might hold a clue. When their stories are uncovered, they will be told.

Part II - The Research

1

The Tripp Family in Southeastern New England

Most of the Tripps in southern New England descend from John Tripp of Lincolnshire, England who was born about 1611. In England, he was apprenticed as a ship carpenter and immigrated with his master to Boston about 1635. In 1638 John fled with a later master to Rhode Island to avoid religious persecution. His apprenticeship must have ended soon after that as he married Mary Paine about 1639, probably in Portsmouth, Rhode Island, though no record survived.

John Tripp, "Gentleman," was admitted Freeman of the colony in 1641 which gave him landholding and voting rights. In 1670, Tripp filed a deposition with the court where he stated his age, place of birth, and life history. This deposition was housed at the New Bedford Public Library Genealogy Department.

He made his will in December 1677 and it was probated in October the following year, shortly after his death. His wife Mary survived him, and, as his widow, married Benjamin Engell four years later. She died in Portsmouth in 1687. John and Mary Tripp left five daughters and five sons, all of whom established their own homesteads in the towns from Portsmouth, Rhode Island to Dartmouth, Massachusetts. A large number of their descendants remained in this area for generations while others followed the westward migration track.

My intuition told me that my own ancestral connection to the Tripp family helped Joe Tripp find me, hoping I would be able to help him. On the maternal side of my own family tree I have four lines of descent from John and Mary (Paine) Tripp, one from their daughter Alice, who was born in Portsmouth about 1650 and married William Hall, and three lines that descend from their son Joseph Tripp, who was born in Portsmouth about 1644 and married Mehitable Fish in Dartmouth in 1667.

My closest ancestor with the Tripp name was Sarah Tripp, my fifth great-grandmother, born in 1765, died in 1858, and married to Philip Davis. They lived in Westport, in the area known as Acoaxet. Although Sarah is seven generations removed from me, some of that Tripp blood and DNA are still carried forward in my genetic legacy, as it would have been for Joe Tripp as well.

For those who have done at least some genealogy research, this will all make perfect sense. To those who haven't and aren't familiar with family trees and lineages, it might sound like one confusing mess. Trust me that it isn't, and it became significant in my search for Joe Tripp.

2

The Search through Census and Civil War Records

If Joe Tripp joined the army in 1861, he obviously appeared somewhere in the 1860 United States Census.

A quick search of the index yielded twelve persons indexed with the name of Joseph Tripp (or some variation of either name) in the geographic area I was concerned with, ten in Bristol County and two in Barnstable County. These individuals lived in New Bedford, Fairhaven, Westport, and Yarmouth. There was no one with that name living in Plymouth County or in Newport County. Only five of the twelve were of an age to serve in the War of the Rebellion, the youngest being fifteen along with two sixteen year olds, a seventeen year old, and a twenty-six year old, all in Bristol County. The others were aged fifty-one, sixty, sixty-one and eighty-two years, along with three infants, and these I discounted for my purposes.

The National Park Service maintained an online website with a significant amount of information about all facets of the Civil War. There's a collection of articles discussing the pre-war background and war time experiences, along with descriptions of key places and people. Most importantly for my work, the site included a searchable database of the soldiers and sailors of the Civil War with information about the men who served on both sides, the Union and the Confederacy.

Since Bristol County is located in southern New England, I had no doubt that Joe was a Union soldier. My search in the database produced a list of nineteen records in all of the country of men named Joseph Tripp who served in the war, which included seven records from Massachusetts. Fortunately, I was able to search for records specifically from each state, and found that some of these were for the same person with different enlistment, muster, or regiment transfer dates. A review and comparison of these records yielded a final result of thirteen men named Joseph Tripp who served in the War of the Rebellion, all of them in the Union Army, including four men who served from Massachusetts, all from Bristol County. These four Joseph Tripps were listed in *Massachusetts Soldiers, Sailors, and Marines in the Civil War*, and were also among those found in the 1860 census.

I've provided the specific company history for each of these soldiers to give an idea of the battles and fighting they endured during their enlistment.

Joseph H. Tripp, private, residence Westport. Twenty-second Regiment Massachusetts Volunteer Infantry, Company C. Age eighteen. Occupation farmer. Enlisted and mustered September 2, 1861. Died of disease June 18, 1862, Gaines' Mill, Virginia.

The Twenty-second Regiment arrived in Washington D.C. on October 11, 1861 and was assigned to Hall's Hill, Virginia as part of the defense of Washington, arriving there on October 18. Soon after their arrival, they began rigorous training as skirmishers, which would become the unit's specialty. Skirmishers were infantry or cavalry soldiers stationed ahead or alongside a larger body of friendly troops, usually placed in a skirmish line to harass the enemy.

The following year, from March 10 to 23, they advanced on Manassas, moved on to Alexandria, and then to Fortress Monroe, all in Virginia. They were engaged in their first action during the Peninsular Campaign at Warwick Road near Yorktown on April 5. The unit was involved in the siege of Yorktown from April 5 to May 4. They moved to Hanover Court House, where they were involved from May 27 to 29. Following that engagement, the regiment marched toward Richmond, arriving about June 25, and were based there until July 1.

In Richmond they were in the middle of the Seven Days Battle as Confederate General Robert E. Lee made a fierce push to move the Union Army away from the city. They saw action at Mechanicsville on June 26, and at the battle of Gaines' Mill on June 27. They were then at Harrison's Landing during July to August 15. These latter two locations are given as the place of Joseph's death on the official records, but both engagements were after the date he died.

Three of Joseph's friends, all Westport residents and around his own age, enlisted with him. George A. Gifford, age sixteen, and William R. Macomber, age sixteen, were mustered into Company C on the same day as Joseph, and Peleg W. P. Reed, age seventeen, joined them two weeks later.

Reviewing the list of other soldiers in this Company with Joseph and his mates, I found the name of Charles T. Dale. He enlisted as a private on October 4, 1861. His enlistment record stated he was eighteen years old, had the occupation of engraver, and lived in Taunton, Massachusetts, only twenty-two miles from Westport. According to the official record, he was killed at Yorktown, Virginia on June 15, 1862 and buried in Yorktown National Cemetery. The Regiment was at Yorktown in April, and was in camp at Gaines' Mill on the date attributed to his death, a distance of over 60 miles apart, so it seems if he was killed at Yorktown, he died sometime in April not in June. Regardless, if he was killed at Yorktown, it certainly fit for this young man to be Joe's friend Charlie, whose death during battle Joe described to me in his message.

Joseph was born in Tiverton, Rhode Island on December 21, 1843, the son of Preserved and Lydia (Petty) Tripp. There is no record of his birth there, the date being calculated from the age given on his death record. In some online family trees, though without source documentation, the initial "H" of his middle name is said to stand for "Howland," a family with roots back to the earliest days of Plymouth colony and well-established in the southern Bristol County area.

Joseph had two siblings—Nancy A. Tripp born 1847 and Cyrus Wheeler Tripp born 1853. Joseph was probably named for his paternal grandfather, also Joseph Tripp. Joseph's body was buried in Beech Grove Cemetery, Westport. His father filed application for a pension based on Joseph's service in the War on December 13, 1880.

The death record in Westport for Joseph stated he died of Typhoid Fever on June 18, 1862 at Harrison's Landing, Virginia, age eighteen years five months and twenty-eight days. Additional research revealed that Joseph died at the General Field Hospital at Harrison's Landing. His commander reported he took sick while on a march near New Bridge on the Chickahominy River before they reached Gaines' Mill. His friend William Macomber died of Typhoid Fever on June 14, just four days before Joseph succumbed to the disease, reportedly in camp near Gaines' Mill.

Typhoid Fever was one of the most terrible and feared epidemic diseases in the 1800s and was often fatal. During the Civil War there were well over 75,000 diagnosed cases in Union soldiers and more than 27,000 of them died. An intestinal infection spread by food or water contaminated with the Salmonella bacteria, Typhoid is excreted in urine and fecal matter and can be spread by flies. These conditions were rampant in Union camps during the Civil War.

Patients with severe Typhoid experienced persistent high fever and overwhelming generalized malaise as the bacteria spread through the body, as well as the appearance of red skin lesions called "rose spots." Abdominal distention with accompanying diarrhea or constipation occurred frequently, sometimes causing perforation of the intestine which often led to death. Typhoid could also cause bronchitis, leading to pneumonia. Other symptoms could include lack of appetite, headache, red flushing of the face, and nosebleed. Patients usually demonstrated diminished mental function which included delusions, delirium, and erratic behavior. There were no effective treatments for Typhoid and those who became infected suffered greatly, even if they did survive.

Peleg Reed, the last of the friends to enlist, received a disability discharge on October 16, 1862 at Sharpsburg, Maryland and was reported to have died of consumption, the old-fashioned name for tuberculosis, in Washington, D.C. sixteen days later on November 1.

The symptoms of consumption often mimicked those of Typhoid Fever, and during the early part of the war men were often given this diagnosis, with the true cause of the symptoms being Typhoid.

The lone survivor of the four comrades, George Gifford was honorably discharged on October 17, 1864 and returned home to Westport. He was wounded by gunshot at Gettysburg in July 1863 and wounded again near Spotsylvania Court House, Virginia in May 1864. He never married and died in Westport on March 21, 1911, chronically suffering for the rest of his life from the excruciating effects of his two wounds.

This Joseph H. Tripp of Westport who died in Virginia during the war presumably should be ruled out as the once-living identity of my Spirit. However, he seemed to fit almost every aspect of the description given by the Spirit Joe Tripp, except for the means of his death. But, barring any other circumstances, I felt that had to be the crucial factor for identification. If he died in Virginia of disease, he couldn't be the same man who accidentally killed himself a few years later. The other three Joseph Tripps, therefore, had to be fully researched to determine if they could have been the man who became the Spirit of my Joe Tripp.

Joseph F. Tripp, private, residence Taunton. Fourth Regiment Mass. Volunteer Infantry, Company K. Age twenty-seven. Occupation painter. Enlisted September 15, 1862, mustered in September 23, 1862.

The Fourth Regiment was organized in Lakeville, Massachusetts in September 1862, moved to New York in December and then to New Orleans and Carrollton, Louisiana in January to February 1863. They moved on to other Louisiana sites in March through June where they took part in the siege and assault on Port Hudson on June 14 and then in the fighting for Brashear City on June 23. Tripp was taken prisoner at Brashear City, but was paroled just three days later. The Regiment served garrison duty at Port Hudson after its surrender on July 9 to August 4. They were then shipped from Louisiana to Cairo, Illinois by steamer boat, and then by rail to Boston, arriving August 17. Tripp and the entire regiment were mustered out on August 28, 1863.

Joseph F. Tripp of Taunton was born in Fairhaven (according to his marriage record) in 1834, the son of Pardon and Sarah (Macomber) Tripp. Pardon was of Fairhaven and Sarah was of Westport at the time of their marriage in 1823. In the 1850 United States Census, Joseph was listed with his parents and siblings living in Fairhaven. The family consisted of his father, Pardon Tripp age fifty, a cooper (barrel maker), his mother Sarah F. age fifty-six, sister Sarah E. age eighteen, and brothers Frederick A. age eleven and John D. age ten. Joseph married in Sandwich, Massachusetts on April 4, 1857 to Catherine Tyne.

By the time of the 1860 census, Joseph was living with his young family in Taunton. He was listed as age twenty-six with the occupation of wheelwright, with his wife Catherine and two children, Ella age one and an unnamed female infant age two months. Both of these little girls died of Scarletina in January 1865. In the 1865 Massachusetts state census in Taunton, Joseph and Catherine had only one child living with them, Mary J. age two. They were still living in Taunton in 1870, but his occupation was listed as painter, and there were two children listed in the census, Frank age three and Mary J. age eight. By 1880, the family was living in Cottage City on Martha's Vineyard. Joseph's occupation was still a painter, and another son was added to the family, Albert age 5. On April 9, 1881, Joseph filed an application for a federal pension for his service in the war.

In 1890 a special census was taken to enumerate Civil War Union veterans and their widows, and Joseph was included in the listing for Cottage City with the information that he had served as a private in Company K of the Fourth Massachusetts Infantry from 1862 to 1863. This was the solid piece of information that connected this Joseph to the entry for his service from Taunton. Joseph age sixty-three and Catherine age sixty-two were still living in Cottage City in the 1900 census, with unmarried son Frank, age thirty-three, at that date their only surviving child of the seven they had borne. In the 1910 and 1920 census records, Joseph and Catherine were living in Oak Bluffs on Martha's Vineyard. One family tree I found online had a death date for Catherine of 1920 and for Joseph as 16 July 1926 in Vineyard Haven, Martha's Vineyard, but there were no sources listed for these dates. Clearly, this wasn't the man that became the tormented Spirit of Joe Tripp.

Joseph H. Tripp, private, residence New Bedford. Third Regiment Mass. Volunteer Cavalry, Company E. Age forty-four. Occupation farmer. Enlisted and mustered January 5, 1864.

This regiment served in New Orleans and Brashear City, Louisiana and at various sites as part of the Red River Campaign. In July 1864, the regiment was moved to Fortress Monroe, Virginia and Washington, D.C. They were then moved to Maryland and later on to Harper's Ferry, West Virginia. They served as part of Sheridan's Shenandoah Valley Campaign from August 7 to November 28 and saw fighting at a number of sites. They were moved back to Maryland in December 1864.

Tripp was transferred to the Veteran Reserve Corps on January 10, 1865. He mustered out on October 6 that year as part of Company E Ninth VRC. The Veteran Reserve Corps was originally called the Invalid Corps and was a military organization within the Union Army that gave light duty to partially disabled or otherwise infirm soldiers or former soldiers. This allowed more able-bodied soldiers to serve in combat. About 60,000 men served in the Reserves. They performed guard duty, did patrol duty at Washington D.C., and enforced the draft.

This older Joseph H. Tripp was a little more difficult to find and figure out. His record indicated he was age forty-four when he enlisted in 1864 and was a farmer with a residence in New Bedford. I couldn't find a Joseph Tripp that age, born about 1820, in any of the census records or vital records for New Bedford or the surrounding towns. Since he was quite a bit older than the nineteen years that I got in the message from the Spirit Joe Tripp, I doubted he was the right person, but I wanted to make sure this supposition was correct. I decided to approach this mystery with an elimination method. I compared all the records I collected on all the Joseph Tripps I found, even those who didn't serve in the Civil War at all. After accomplishing this task, a few records were left over and, as I reviewed them again, I identified details that linked them together.

In the 1860 census for New Bedford, Joseph H. Tripp was enumerated with a woman of the same surname, Theresa A., probably his wife, and two other apparently unrelated women, perhaps boarders. They lived in the 4th ward of the city when the census was taken on June 30. Joseph was noted to be fifty-one years old, born in Massachusetts, and a laborer. His wife Theresa was twenty-six years old and also born in Massachusetts. This gave Joseph a birth year of about 1809.

Another entry in the 1860 census for New Bedford in the 2nd Ward, taken on August 7, listed Joseph Tripp, age forty-five, and his wife Thersa [sic], age forty. Joseph's occupation was noted as laborer, and both were born in Massachusetts. Since Theresa wasn't a commonly used woman's name in that area and time period, I felt comfortable this was the same couple, moved to another dwelling between June 30 and August 7, and therefore were enumerated twice in the same census. I also began to see this Joseph wasn't consistent reporting his age in all situations. Of course, someone other than Joseph or Theresa might have reported the information to the census taker, in which case ages could have been a complete guess. This was far from an unusual occurrence. I checked the 1870 and 1880 census for New Bedford, for all of Massachusetts, and finally for the whole country, but there was no Joseph Tripp with wife Theresa anywhere to be found in the census for these years.

That led me to consider a death record I found for a Joseph H. Tripp who died in New Bedford on May 23, 1869, age fifty-nine. This would calculate to a birth year of 1809 or 1810. The record noted he was a farmer, born in Westport, and died in his own house in New Bedford of Lung Fever. The spaces for marital status and parents' names were blank. I initially connected this death to the earlier 1860 census record because of the age, but hadn't considered that it might belong to the Civil War soldier who was supposed to be ten years younger.

I found the marriage record for Joseph with Theresa A. Wing, in New Bedford on January 22, 1864, two and a half weeks after he enlisted in the army but almost four years after the 1860 census where Joseph and Theresa Tripp were enumerated together with the same surname, not just once but twice. In the marriage record, he gave his age as forty-eight (born 1816), and stated he was a farmer, born in Westport, the son of Jonathan and Ellis (Alice) Tripp, and that this was his second marriage. Theresa gave her age as twenty-eight, born in Rochester, Massachusetts, and this was her first marriage.

Joseph's story seemed to be a bit more complex than anticipated, but I believed I was on the right track. Learning from the marriage record that Joseph was married previously, I searched for him in the 1850 census. I found Joseph H. Tripp, age forty-four, farmer, born Massachusetts, resident in Westport. The others in the household were Amy age forty-seven, probably his wife, and their children—Mary A. age twenty, James W. age eighteen, Esquire W. age sixteen, Abraham A. age fourteen, and Emily S. age ten, along with a Sarah W. Macomber age twenty-two. I also found Jonathan and Alice Tripp, Joseph's parents, in the 1850 census in Westport, he at age seventy-two and she at age sixty-three.

A search for a first marriage record for Joseph revealed that he married Amy Kirby. The intentions were filed in Westport December 16, 1826 but I could find no record of the actual marriage. I was able to find a marriage record for their daughter Sarah W. who married

Richmond Macomber in Tiverton in 1850, and was therefore the Sarah W. Macomber with them in the 1850 census. I also found a death record in Westport for their son Abraham in 1904. However, I couldn't find any death for Amy or any death or marriage records for the other children. I came across a couple of family trees online, which gave a death year for Amy of 1854 and added another son Emery born 1827, but there were no sources or evidence for these claims.

It seemed, therefore, that this was probably the Joseph H. of the Civil War record even though the information I found didn't all fit nicely together. There just wasn't any other Joseph H. Tripp living during that time period that could have belonged to even some of the records I found. A marriage intention for his parents, Jonathan Tripp and Alice Devoll, was filed in Westport in February 1804.

Since Joseph married Amy in 1826, his actual birth was probably between 1804 and 1808, despite all the variations he reported, which meant that at the time of his enlistment in the army in 1864 he was at least fifty-six years old. Perhaps that was the reason he reported a younger age, afraid he wouldn't be allowed to enlist if they knew how old he actually was. Why did he want to enlist at that age at all? Why did Joseph and Theresa finally decide to marry two weeks following his enlistment after four years of co-habitation? I found no information to answer those questions. I haven't found any further record for Theresa after their marriage in 1864 so I don't know what happened to her. I can't find her listed in the Massachusetts 1865 census.

Although I couldn't correlate what I knew about this Joseph H. Tripp with the story that Spirit Joe Tripp related, I sensed this older Joseph was also a tormented soul and that his last days on this earth weren't peaceful or easy ones. I believe he died alone, both his wives gone, and his surviving children estranged from him. Whoever reported his death didn't even know enough about him to provide a full accounting of his most vital personal information. I wasn't sure why I felt so sad about these circumstances, as I never connected with his

Spirit directly, but I felt sure this was true. He wasn't the Joe Tripp who killed himself in the woods that day, but he too needed to have his story told, and perhaps I'll pursue it further one day.

Joseph Tripp, private, residence Fairhaven. First Regiment Mass. Volunteer Cavalry, Company K. Age nineteen. Occupation mariner. Enlisted October 5, 1861, mustered October 9, 1861.

Company K in Third Battalion was detained at New York until January 13, 1862, then sent to Hilton Head, South Carolina as part of the force under General Thomas West Sherman. They saw action at Pocotaligo, South Carolina on May 22. From July 1862 until August 4, 1863, they operated on the South Carolina Coast as a detached battalion. In August the unit was permanently detached and made an independent battalion. They were on expedition to St. John's Bluff, Florida September 30 to October 13 and again on expedition to Pocotaligo, October 21 to 23. During the latter part of the winter of 1863-64, they were operating in Florida, being engaged February 10 at Barber's Place near Lake City with a loss of one killed and eleven wounded. The battalion was still in Florida when by Special Order #70 of the War Department dated February 12, 1864, the battalion was transferred to the Fourth Massachusetts Cavalry becoming the 1st Battalion of that regiment.

At the time of transfer to the Fourth Mass. Cavalry, Joseph was age twenty-three and had re-enlisted on January 1, 1864. This battalion was engaged in action at Olustee, Florida on February 20, losing six men wounded. On May 8, the First Battalion arrived at Bermuda Hundred, located outside of Richmond, Virginia, coming from the Department of the South. From May 9 to June 16, they participated in the operations on the Bermuda Hundred front and before Petersburg, Virginia.

Late in May they were assigned to duty at 10th Corps Headquarters along with two companies of the Third Battalion. They engaged in operations on the east front of Petersburg and Richmond throughout the summer and fall of 1864 and the following winter. The First Battalion wasn't actively engaged during the winter of 1864-65. They were mostly assigned to duty at corps headquarters.

For the Spring campaign of 1865, the First Battalion was in Virginia, with Company K specifically on duty at the headquarters of the Twenty-fourth Corps. They participated in the fall of Petersburg on April 2, were at High Bridge and Farmville April 6 to 7, and at Appomattox Court House on April 9 where they witnessed the surrender of General Lee and his army. They then saw duty at Richmond until November when they were discharged. Joseph Tripp was promoted to Corporal on September 25, 1864 and Sergeant on July 1, 1865. He mustered out November 14, 1865 as Quarter Master Sergeant.

Even though this was the last Civil War soldier named Joseph Tripp I found who could possibly be the Spirit Joe Tripp, I really couldn't rely on just the process of elimination of the previous three. I had to find and evaluate all the documentation that would prove this was the person who became the Spirit Joe Tripp who contacted me.

The basic information I gleaned from his Civil War record seemed to fit what the Spirit Joe Tripp related to me. This Joseph Tripp was nineteen years old when he enlisted in 1861 from Fairhaven. One fact that puzzled me was that this soldier said he was a mariner in civilian life. The story I received from the Spirit Joe Tripp gave no hint of this at all, and actually inferred that he was a farmer. This would have to be reconciled as I pursued more documentation. A review of the remaining records I collected pertaining to all Joseph Tripps showed there were a few that appeared to belong to this soldier.

Searching for a Joseph Tripp born about 1842 with a residence in Fairhaven brought me to Joseph, son of Ebenezer Tripp. Ebenezer was a mariner, and I found records of two whaling voyages for him. The first was aboard the Brig *Agenora* which departed Fairhaven on August 5, 1817 headed for Brazil under Master Stanton Burtch, and returned to

Fairhaven on June 8, 1818. On the crew list, Ebenezer was noted to be age thirty-three, dark skin, and resident in Fairhaven. Ebenezer sailed again under Master Burtch on the Ship *Herald* departing Fairhaven on July 21, 1818 for Patagonia and returning to port on April 3, 1819. On the crew list for this voyage Ebenezer was noted to be thirty-four years old, with dark skin and hair, and a resident of Fairhaven.

The next record for Ebenezer was his marriage to Sophronia Bodfish in Fairfield, Maine on May 10, 1841 and the record stated that Ebenezer resided in Fairhaven and Sophronia was from Fairfield. I never found the record of a birth for their son Joseph, but he was probably born the following year in 1842. I also didn't find a record for Sophronia's death, but I believe it was at or shortly after Joseph's birth.

Ebenezer died on February 3, 1849, and his death was recorded in the Fairhaven town records. The record stated that he was deaf and dumb, widowed, and age sixty-four when he died. His occupation was listed as shoemaker and the cause of his death was Inflammation of the Bowel. He was buried in the Village graveyard. His place of birth was noted to be Saybrook, Connecticut and his parents were named as Reuben and Susanna Tripp.

Ebenezer made a will on April 2, 1846, calling himself of Fairhaven and "late a Mariner," which bequeathed all his estate to his son Joseph Tripp. His will stipulated that if Joseph didn't survive him, his estate should go to Ansell Tripp, son of his sister Polly Tripp, with further provision that when Ansell Tripp "ceased to live" the remainder of his estate should go to the children of his sister Susan Gulliver. Ebenezer appointed Nathaniel Church of Fairhaven to be executor.

Three days after Ebenezer's death, on February 6, 1849, Nathaniel Church appeared in Probate Court and posted bond as the Executor of Ebenezer's will, which was entered into probate that date. Church also posted surety bond in court on that same date to be appointed guardian of Ebenezer's son Joseph Tripp of Fairhaven, a minor under the age of fourteen.

Inventory of the estate was presented on May 31, with a total value of $2,477. The inventory included such items as household goods and furniture, farming tools, shoemaker's tools, several notes on hand owed the estate, and 1/32 share in each of two ships. Another inventory of the minor's estate was presented to court on May 1, 1855 which totaled over $3,400. The third and final account of Nathaniel Church as guardian for Joseph Tripp was dated May 6, 1859 and gave a total for the estate at $2,406.95.

In the 1850 census, a year after his father's death, Joseph was living with his Bodfish grandparents, Samuel and Fanny, in Ellisville, Maine, age eight, and born in Massachusetts. In 1855 he was back in Massachusetts listed in the state census as age thirteen and living in the home of his guardian Nathaniel Church in Fairhaven. Joseph wasn't listed in the 1860 census. He wasn't enumerated in the Massachusetts State Census of 1865 as he was with the Army in Virginia until being mustered out in November later that year. I found no listing for him in the census records for 1870 or 1880 in any of the towns of Bristol County, Massachusetts.

Since his occupation was given as mariner, I checked the Whaling Crew Index from the New Bedford Whaling Museum. The online database covered the years 1809-1927, so I expected to find him in the records. There was a total of seventeen records for any Joseph Tripp in the database, with years ranging from 1841 to 1876. Fortunately, the later records from the mid-1850s forward included some descriptive information about each mariner. After eliminating those that were too early or those with descriptions that didn't match what I needed, I came up with five records that all seemed to be for the same Joseph Tripp and were consistent with the information I had.

The earliest crew list record was for Joseph Tripp, age seventeen, departing on the Schooner *Emerald* in 1859. This Joseph had light skin, brown hair, and lived in Fairhaven. Also on the crew list for this voyage was Ansell Tripp, age thirty-eight of Fairhaven. Because of the bequests in Ebenezer's will, I knew Ansell and Joseph were first cousins. Ansell sailed on at least two previous whaling voyages, and since he was about twenty-one years older, probably took Joseph under his wing on his first whaling trip. The *Emerald* departed the port of Fairhaven on May 2, 1859 under Master Thomas F. Lambert and returned in August 1860. This explained why Joseph wasn't listed in the 1860 census, since he was away on a whaling voyage until August of that year and the census in Fairhaven was taken in June.

Joseph next sailed on the Brig *Tekoa* on November 12, 1866, age twenty-three, five feet six inches, light skin, and brown hair, returning to port in August 1868. His next voyage was on the Bark *Tropic Bird* departing November 23, 1868, returning October 1870. On the crew list Joseph was listed as twenty-six, five feet six inches tall, light skin, and brown hair with a residence in Fairhaven. At the time of the 1870 census, taken in June and July of that year, Joseph was away on this whaling voyage, not returning to port in Fairhaven until October.

The last whaling record I found matching this Joseph Tripp was for a voyage in 1871 aboard the Bark *Milwood*. This record gave his age as twenty-nine years, height as five feet six inches, skin light, dark brown hair, and residence in Fairhaven. The *Milwood* sailed from Fairhaven on April 25, 1871 under Master Sanford Stoddard Miner with a destination of Cumberland Inlet, near Baffin Island, Canada. The database information noted the ship was lost in Cumberland Inlet.

In the weekly newspaper *Whaleman's Shipping List and Merchants' Transcript*, published in New Bedford, Tuesday morning September 10, 1872, the shipping list for the latest report on the vessels at sea stated that the bark *Milwood* was lost November 13, 1871 on Black Lead Island in Cumberland Inlet. In the "Letters" column in the same issue, the following was printed:

LOSS OF BARK MILWOOD—Letters from Capt. Milner and Henry C. Hathaway, first mate, late of bark

Milwood, of this port, dated Black Lead Island, Cumberland Inlet, June 28th, report the loss of their vessel, on November 13th, 1871, she having been driven on shore at that island by the ice. She was strained and set to leaking badly, but Capt. Milner had topmasts cut away, which relieved her, and lightened her, when the wind shifted and she came off with 5 feet of water in her hold. Seeing that her pumps could barely keep her free, the Capt. ordered her anchors slipped and she was beached. Everything was saved from the wreck, (including 140 bbls whale oil and a head of bone from a whale which had just been taken,) except the forward ground tier. A survey was held by masters of vessels there, and the vessel was condemned, being found badly strained and unseaworthy. The wreck was then sold for $51. The oil and bone would be shippe[d] home at first opportunity. The crew remained with the officers, organized for whaling during the Winter, but met with no success. Eight of them had shipped in other vessels, and 10 had shipped in the British brig Perseverence, ready to sail for Scotland, full, and the letters probably came by her. The balance of the crew would probably return home on homeward vessels this Fall, or in the steamer chartered by a New London firm to take North provisions for their vessels.

I searched to find what happened to Joseph following this unfortunate turn of events. His name didn't come up in a search on the British Southern Whale Fishery voyage and crew database, which is part of the Whaling History website, so it seems unlikely he joined the crew of the *Perseverence* when it sailed from Cumberland Inlet. From the information I discovered later, he probably joined another ship's crew while on Black Lead Island, or found passage back to another port in the United States where he signed on for another voyage.

Joseph wasn't listed anywhere in the United States in the 1880 census. He was probably out of the country on a whaling voyage. After a good deal of research, I finally found Joseph in California. A Joseph Tripp was listed in the California Great Registers, voter registration lists, living at 26 Silver Street in San Francisco in 1888 and 1890. In the 1888 Register, he was listed as age forty-six, born Massachusetts, occupation Mariner, with a registration date of October 13. In 1890 the entry stated he was age forty-eight, with the rest of the information the same. In the San Francisco City Directory for 1891, Joseph Tripp was listed at the same address, with occupation seaman. It seems Joseph was signing on to whaling voyages, or at least onto merchant ships, from San Francisco.

By 1902, Joseph moved to Vallejo, California, located in the San Francisco Bay area, on San Pablo Bay. I found him in the Directories for the city in 1902, 1904, and 1911 when he was working at the Mare Island Navy Yard. Apparently, his sea-going days were done. He was enumerated in the 1910 census in Vallejo where he lodged in the home of Mary E. Camp at 214 Hospital Street. He was sixty-eight years old, single, and worked as a laborer in the Navy Yard. The entry stated he was born in Massachusetts, his father's birth place was Connecticut, and his mother was born in Maine. This information confirmed that he was the son of Ebenezer and Sophronia.

I found him in the U.S. Civil War Pension Index from the National Archives, stating that he applied for a pension on February 13, 1912 based on service in the First and Fourth Regiments of Cavalry, Company K from Massachusetts, which provided the final proof that this was the same person as the Civil War soldier from Fairhaven.

Joseph died on February 24, 1917 in Napa County, according to the California Death Index. With the information from the index, I obtained a copy of his death certificate. According to that record, he died in the Veterans Home in Yountville, California at age seventy-four of Chronic Endocarditis, Arteriosclerosis, and Senility. His birthplace was given as Massachusetts, and his parents' full names were recorded. His occupation was listed as laborer in the Navy Yard, and his former residence as Vallejo, California. He was buried in the Veterans Home Cemetery.

Administration of his estate was assigned to B. F. Kotz, Public Administrator for Solano County, California on April 9, 1917. Joseph died without a will, still had a legal residence in Vallejo in Solano County, and owned property in Richmond, Contra Costa County. The probate records stated there were no known heirs to his estate, and Joseph had no personal property. Following inventory and appraisal of the real estate, it was sold on December 31, 1917 for $250. The fees and claims placed on the estate totaled $251.12.

After a life filled with adversity and adventure, this Joseph Tripp died alone and penniless. His is certainly a story worthy of telling, but he obviously wasn't the Spirit Joe Tripp who came to me in such distress.

Since none of these four men fit the facts for my Spirit Joe Tripp, I expanded my search parameters. I made a list of all the Civil War soldiers from the target geographic area, starting with those named Tripp first. If he went by a different name, intuition told me his surname was Tripp either with the nickname Joe or a different given name all together. I thought I could sort through them, first ruling out some based on age or other details and then checking census and death records for the rest.

Besides the four Josephs I already dealt with, there were fifty-three other men with the surname Tripp from the southern area of Bristol, Barnstable and Plymouth Counties. Of these, five of them served exclusively in the Navy. I put these aside for future reference if needed, but the story I received from Joe Tripp was clearly infantry or artillery, fought on land.

Most towns reported one or two except for New Bedford with twenty-three soldiers, Westport with ten, and Fairhaven with five.

Nearby Dartmouth had only one Tripp soldier to its credit. These towns were my primary target area, being closest to where I was contacted by the Spirit in Westport. Of the total thirty-nine men for these four towns, four were in the Navy and eight died during the war prior to discharge, either of disease or being killed in action. That brought my search group down to twenty-seven. I eliminated any one of them who was age thirty or older at enlistment. That left me with ten from New Bedford, two from Fairhaven and five from Westport, all seventeen of them in their teens or twenties. This was the next group I would start searching to find my Joe Tripp.

Once again, I went through the process, using census records, vital records for birth, marriage and deaths, burial records, and any other records I thought would be helpful. In the end, none of these Tripps from the target geographic group could have been my Spirit Joe Tripp.

I went back over the list of Tripps from the other towns of Bristol and Plymouth Counties. After culling those who were over age thirty or who were killed or died during the war, I was left with eight men who lived in five different towns—Swansea, Taunton, Mattapoisett, Wareham, and Dennis. I managed to find birth and death records for all of them, ranging from 1893 to 1941. All of them died from chronic disease or at an advanced age. None of them were my Spirit Joe Tripp.

3

Overseers of the Poor and The Westport Almshouse

Government jurisdiction of overseeing the care of the poor was originally established in England around the turn of the seventeenth century, and continued in the colonies. In Massachusetts, the care and support of poor persons was deemed the responsibility of the town, under the auspices of the Overseers of the Poor, with each town taking care of its own residents. Most often these poor were widowed women and orphaned children or at times disabled men. To prevent transients from using the limited resources available in each town, there were strict investigations into the origin of individuals and whether they belonged to the town, often determined by the parents' or grandparents' place of abode and whether they were tax-paying residents.

In the mid-1800s, the construction of Almshouses began, partly to accommodate the large influx of immigrants, and the Overseers took on the responsibility for managing them as well. The majority of information in the Westport records was correspondence sent to and received from other towns, requesting information or confirmation of the poor person's legitimate place of residence to establish which town was responsible for the care and support of that person.

The earliest Almshouse register in Westport started in 1860, and the Overseers on March 26 were noted as Ezra P. Brownell, Restcome Macomber, and H. W. Kirby. The Keeper of the Almshouse was G. E. Brownell. The register was a listing of the paupers that held a residence for any length of time within the confines of the Almshouse, starting with those who already resided there in March 1860 and proceeding chronologically through the register pages. The information recorded included the name, place of residence when admitted, age when admitted, gender of the individual, date of admission, and a space for discharge notes that generally included the date of discharge, whether by departure or death, the condition at departure and whose care they were discharged to, whether they returned and a return date, or a cause of death and where buried.

In the majority of cases, the bodies of those who died at the Almshouse were claimed by a family member to be buried in a family burial ground or cemetery plot. There were some buried as paupers in the Potter's Field in Beech Grove Cemetery. The earliest of these recorded in the Westport Almshouse register was William Briggs, buried in Row One, Grave 13 on October 20, 1860. There were burials in Potter's Field previous to the starting date of the register, but there was no record of those. Following down the list of names through the successively dated pages, it was easy to discern the pattern of burials that the overseers followed. Each body was buried in the next consecutive open grave, moving from the first row to the corresponding numbered grave in the second row. "Unknown" (as I was now thinking of him/her) was buried in the second row, grave 25.

With a quick browse through the list of records, I managed to find the page in the Overseers' Journal that the information was taken from for the Unknown burial in the website database. The page contained a map of the paupers' gravesites, which were laid out in two long rows of 36 graves each and numbered consecutively from 1 to 36 in each row. There was a list of seven names with their grave numbers including the notation for "25 Unknown Taken from School House Lot." This was the same note recorded on the town cemetery website. There was nothing else to learn from the entry, other than the mapped location of the grave.

After studying the information, I determined an approximate date of burial of Unknown's remains from the other names on the list. In the first row were Frank Hearn, Catherine Hearn, and Margaret A. Hearn. These names weren't in the register of the Almshouse residents, so no dates of death or burial were recorded there for any of them. Checking the death records for the town, I found that they were the children of Richard and Margaret Hearn and they all died within eighteen days. Frank was twenty-eight days old and died on August 13, 1884, buried in the first row grave 25, presumably just before Unknown. Catherine died on August 23 at two years old and was buried in the first row grave 26, likely just after Unknown. I checked other burials just before and after these to confirm the dates. The third sibling Margaret died on September 1 and was buried first row grave 27.

I found no identified burials in the Almshouse register for graves 26 or 27 in the second row, and there were no names on the list for these graves. Grave 28 in the first row was allotted to James Dolman, a two-month-old infant who died on September 29, 1884, not an Almshouse resident. The burial in the second row grave 24 next to Unknown on the other side was for Margaret Durtz who was an inmate at the Almshouse and died on August 29, 1883. If the burial of Unknown followed the usual pattern, the remains were buried in the second row grave 25 between the dates of the burials of Frank and Catherine Hearn, from August 13 to August 23, 1884. The outside possible range seemed to be between August 29, 1883 and September 29, 1884.

Now I had good estimate of a one year time period when the remains of Unknown were brought from the School House lot and buried in Potter's Field in Beech Grove Cemetery.

4

School House No. 7 and The Davis Family Connection

By looking closely at a number of maps posted on the Westport Historical Documents website, I found one dated 1858 which identified each school by number. School House No. 7 was in the area that included the upper reaches of the West Branch of the Westport River, also known as the Acoaxet River. School House No. 7 was located on what is now Cornell Road at the intersection with Main Road. According to historical maps from the period of the 1830s to the 1850s, the area was sparsely settled with large tracts of wooded, undeveloped land. There were several Tripp families that lived in the area according to these maps.

Using census records, I determined that the burial ground near the school house was located on the family homestead of one particular Davis family, originally Benjamin Davis and later his son George Washington Davis. By 1810, there were some Tripp families living in the nearby area—Thomas Tripp, William Tripp, and John Tripp. I searched through the town land and probate records to gather information on Benjamin and his son.

For some reason, after finding the probate records for Benjamin, I felt strongly that I needed to check the Westport Town records again. Intuition or premonition, I never ignored these psychic directives. Not exactly sure what it was I was supposed to look for, I started with tax records. The earliest records online were for 1787, and Benjamin Davis was included along with several other Davis men, William, Stephen, Nathan, Job, and John (noted as Job's son). I then looked at the records for Town Accounts, which included listings of individuals who acquired debts on behalf of the town and for whom payments were authorized.

There were a number of entries for Benjamin Davis and also for William Davis. In May 1796, $6.11 was paid to William Davis Esq. and Benjamin Davis together for sundries provided. In May 1802, Benjamin Davis was paid $14.91 due on the books of the store for necessities delivered to Sal Earle in the year 1795. This information about a store was new to me. I found Benjamin and William mentioned in a number of other town records, and in 1792 William Davis Esq. was a selectman for the town.

I checked the database on the town cemetery website. There was a William Davis Burial Ground on Cornell Road, not far from the corner with Main Road, that abutted the property where School House No. 7 was located. This was next to the area I believed was the property of Benjamin and George W. Davis, where George and his family and Unknown were originally buried.

According to the town's description, the William Davis Burial Ground contained nine marked gravestones and no unmarked stones. Those buried in the cemetery were William Davis Esquire and his wife Margaret, Philip Davis and his wife Sarah, William Thomas Davis (son of Philip) and his wife Ruth, Charles R. Davis son of William T., Margaret G. Davis daughter of William T., and Mary D. Davis daughter of Preserved Davis. Of these individuals, I already knew of three besides the elder William. William Thomas Davis was the prudential officer for School District No. 7, and his parents, Philip and Sarah Davis, who I believed were my fifth great-grandparents.

There wasn't simply a Tripp familial connection in my own family tree, an ancestry shared with Joe Tripp. I now shared a Davis familial connection with Unknown. From the gravestone inscription, I knew a birth and death date for William Davis, Esquire. I checked for probate records for him. This is when the reason for this psychic premonition became perfectly clear.

William Davis of Westport wrote his will on April 27, 1797. He gave his wife Margaret the improvement of one third of his real estate, four good milk cows, and one good riding mare, together with all the household goods not otherwise disposed of, in lieu of her dower and power of thirds. He gave to his loving brother Stephen Davis and Stephen's son Philip Davis all his wearing apparel to be equally divided between them.

He bequeathed to his brother Benjamin Davis and Benjamin's son George Washington Davis "all the interest & property I have in Trade in company with him the s[ai]d Benjamin." Benjamin and George were to pay and fulfill all the contracts for the company and give his wife any payment for the stock of cheese and beef that was delivered to the store the previous fall. They also received the store and the lot of land on which it stood, as well as a lot of land called the Sill house.

William gave his brother Aaron his black horse. He gave a colt to David Howland, son of Humphrey Howland. He bequeathed to his grandson William Thomas Davis, son of Philip Davis, and his nephew William Davis, son of Aaron Davis, all the rest of his estate, both real and personal. William's wife Margaret and his brothers Benjamin and Aaron were named executors, and he signed as William Davis Esquire. The will was submitted for probate on June 7, 1797.

William's will clearly outlined the family relationships and put everything in perspective for me. I was amazed. I now knew that Philip Davis, my fifth great-grandfather was the nephew of William and Benjamin and, according to the will, his father was their brother Stephen Davis. Many years previously, I had proven my ancestry back to Philip and his wife Sarah Tripp, through their daughter Nancy, who married Pardon Sherman in Westport in 1814. For some reason, at the time I decided my ancestor Philip was the son of Jonathan Davis and his wife Sarah Taber who had a son named Philip born a few years later. That Philip married another Sarah Taber.

After reading William's will, I knew without a doubt my earlier presumption was incorrect. For many years, I claimed the wrong ancestors and their ancestral line back several generations, although both lines traced back to the same original colonial ancestor. I never would have questioned this or discovered the truth if I wasn't researching the spirit of Joe Tripp, Unknown from the Davis family burial ground, and the Skeleton in the woods. I believed, without any doubt, there was a familial blood connection between me and these spirits, and they were guiding me along this path.

I researched the antecedents of this Davis family, my own family as well as being the connection with Unknown. Checking my notes, I realized I never looked at the actual death record of Philip Davis, probably because I worked on that family line long before the internet and digitalization of documents. When I found an online copy of his death record in Westport in 1859, his parents were listed as "Stephen & Piece" Davis. A check of the records in Dartmouth showed intentions to marry filed by Stephen Davis, son of Aaron Davis, and Peace Maccumber, daughter of Philip Maccumber, on May 10, 1760. That gave me one more generation back to Aaron Davis. Stephen was the brother of William named in his will.

In Southeastern Massachusetts and nearby Rhode Island towns, Aaron was a common name in the Davis family as the earliest known immigrant ancestor and family progenitor was Aaron Davis, born about 1640 and married to Mary, whose maiden name was unknown. Aaron first settled in Newport, Rhode Island and was listed as a proprietor of Dartmouth in 1694. In 1698 he was ordained as the minister of the First Baptist Church of Dartmouth. He was a mason by trade, and died probably in Dartmouth about 1713.

Aaron and Mary had a son Aaron Jr. and are also thought to be the parents of sons William, Joshua, Samuel, and John. Aaron Jr. was born in Newport in 1670 and died in Little Compton in 1730, had a wife named Mary, and children Sarah, Abigail, Mary, Elizabeth, and William. The line I originally and mistakenly thought to be my Davis family was Philip son of Jonathan, son of William, son of Aaron Jr., son of Aaron, original proprietor. William and Benjamin were commonly used names through many generations of the family.

I found a will that belonged to my newly identified ancestor, Aaron Davis, the father of William, Benjamin, Stephen, and Aaron of Westport, written May 5, 1771. In the will he named his "Loving and well beloved wife Mary" who he referred to as the mother of his children. He made bequests to his four sons and to two daughters, Abigail Davis and Ellenor Davis. Aaron then directed his four sons to provide for and take care of his sister Elizabeth Davis.

Aaron divided his farm and homestead land among his four sons, and stated he received this land, by gift and deed, from his father. One of the abutters to the property named in the will was George Tripp. Son William Davis was appointed executor. The will was witnessed by Stephen Tripp, Philip Taber, and Philip Tripp and presented to the probate court on November 11, 1771 along with the inventory of his estate. Obviously, there was a close tie with the Tripp family in that area.

The Court previously ordered the inventory on September 23 and it was taken on October 2 with a total value of £708 (the British pound being the standard currency of the time prior to independence from Britain in 1776). On October 22, son Aaron appeared before the Court and chose his mother Mary to be his guardian, as he was a minor at age fourteen. Mary paid a bond of £1,000. She signed the bond with her mark of an "X" and it was also signed by William Davis and Philip Tripp, with witness signatures of Stephen Davis and Job Hodges.

There was an Aaron Davis whose birth was recorded in Dartmouth on July 29, 1712 with Benjamin Davis as father. There were two other Aarons in the Dartmouth records, but the dates, marriages, and children's records ruled them out. The birth date of this Aaron, son of Benjamin, was within range for him to be the father of William, Stephen, Benjamin, and Aaron. Besides Aaron, the births of four daughters for Benjamin were listed in the Dartmouth records – Mary born 1710, Hannah born 1715, Abigail born 1717, and Elizabeth born 1726. The birth of this sister Elizabeth supported that this was the same Aaron Davis, who named his sister Elizabeth in his will. The mother's name wasn't given for any of these births. Benjamin had to be born no later than 1690, and must have married about 1708-1709.

Benjamin Davis, yeoman of Dartmouth, wrote his will on March 18, 1750. He bequeathed to his well-beloved wife Ellenor two good cows, his feather bed, and "chest of draws." She was to have the use and improvements of the dwelling house and all indoor moveables, along with a privilege to the orchard to gather as many apples as she wanted. His son Aaron was to provide for his mother, giving her all the provisions she might need during her lifetime as long as she remained a widow. He gave Aaron all the remainder of his old homestead that he hadn't given to him previously, along with his desk "where I keep my Rightings," and all his wearing apparel.

He bequeathed a sum of money to his three grandchildren who were the children of his deceased daughter Mary Soule. Benjamin gave his daughter Abigail Tripp, wife of George Tripp, the sum of twenty pounds and the great brass kettle after her mother passed. Daughter Elizabeth Davis would receive five shillings. Abigail and Elizabeth along with granddaughter Hannah Soule were to have all the remainder of the household goods that weren't otherwise disposed of. Here was another Tripp connection. This identified George Tripp, named as a neighbor to Aaron's property in his will, as his brother-in-law, the husband of his sister Abigail Davis.

I wasn't able to prove the parents of Benjamin Davis, with a birth date about 1685-1690. Clearly, he was related to the family of Aaron Davis Sr., though he wasn't the son of Aaron Jr. who was born about 1670. There were no records that linked Benjamin to any of Aaron Jr.'s identified brothers. I didn't find any birth or marriage records that seemed to belong to Benjamin, and the maiden name of his wife Eleanor was unknown. The more I researched this Davis family, however, the more connections I found to the Tripp family as close neighbors with family inter-marriages.

Moving forward in time to the burial ground on the Davis property on Cornell Road, George Washington Davis Sr. still lived in Westport and was enumerated in the 1820 census again as Washington Davis. His wife, two sons and three daughters were all accounted for. I couldn't find any listing for George in 1830, but his son George Jr. was living in New Bedford. In 1840, George Sr. was again listed in Westport, with only his wife and him in the home.

A notice was published in the *New Bedford Mercury* newspaper offering for sale "the well-known farm" of George W. Davis in Westport "situated on the main road leading from Head of Westport River to the Point, two miles from the Point and one from either branch of the Westport River." This was the location I determined near School House No. 7. The sale notice described the farm as consisting of fifty-five acres of pasture, meadow land and orchards, and "well-watered." The property contained a two-story dwelling house, barn, and other out-buildings. The sales agents were listed as George W. Davis Jr. and Benjamin Davis (the two sons of George W. Davis Sr.). The notice included a post-script that if the farm wasn't previously disposed of, it would be sold at public auction on Monday, November 29, 1847. Apparently, George was in no condition to continue to manage the farm and live alone after his wife died, and his sons needed to dispose of it, having homes and property of their own.

I found the deed for sale of this Davis property in Westport. George W. Jr. and brother Benjamin Davis, along with John Allen sold it to Gideon Brightman for $2000 on December 1, 1847, quite a substantial sum for the time. The abutters to the property were named as Nathaniel Potter, Stephen Cornell, William Hicks, Allen Davis, and Restcome Manchester. The deed reserved the right for paving and repaving the lane that went through the lot leading to Allen Davis's property, but there was no mention of the family burial ground where George's wife Hannah and their daughter Sarah were buried.

By the time of the 1850 census, George was living with his son Benjamin in New Bedford, listed as a farmer, age seventy-four. George died September 21, 1852 in Worcester, Massachusetts, although his death was recorded in the New Bedford city death records. He died of consumption.

George's daughter Sarah died previously in New Bedford in 1829, and his wife Hannah died there in 1846. George buried them both on his property in Westport. He went to live with his son in New Bedford after Hannah's death, and he too was laid to rest in the family burial plot in 1852, after it was sold. The graves of this family remained intact on the property until 1884 even though it was sold outside of the family. I speculated that the Davis family may have given a piece of their land to the town to build the school, and so technically the burial ground was no longer a part of the Davis homestead property, though I found no documented evidence of this.

I went back to the Westport town historical website, and combed through the records once again. I found several references to Aaron Davis (1712-1771), his father Benjamin Davis, and Aaron's four sons. These confirmed the location of the Davis family homestead in the Acoaxet area of Dartmouth, later Westport. Although there was no way to determine a connection, I found a land survey of the homestead of an earlier Aaron Davis, in the Dartmouth Proprietors' Land Book, dated September 23, 1712. I believe this was either the father or a brother of the elder Benjamin. This Davis homestead was in the same locale as the Davis property of these later generations, including Aaron and his four sons.

What I didn't find, though, was what I was really looking for, some reference, however slight, to the burial of the skeletal remains that were found by Detective Oesting in 1876.

I decided to spend some time at the Westport Library and see if anything more was available there than online. I was pleased to discover that the library had a designated room housing a large collection of town and local history documents and references. It was nice to find once again that Westport considered the efforts to preserve its history of significant value. My first priority was to look at the maps to see if there were any that weren't posted to the website. All the maps were labeled and indexed, so it was easy to find a few that I hadn't already reviewed. One in particular which identified the lots of the earliest landowners seemed to be helpful.

First and foremost, these maps confirmed that the Davis and Tripp families were neighbors in the Acoaxet area. It was useful to put the lots of land belonging to the various residents of the area in perspective graphically, to see whose lands abutted and who the immediate neighbors were. One map was particularly helpful, and though it wasn't dated, the caption written along the bottom stated "Shows Early Landowners." The hand-drawn map outlined the boundaries of each lot and the owner's name was hand-printed inside the boundary lines. Benjamin Davis' name was in two adjacent lots, abutted by Stephen Wilcox and Ichabod Potter on the south, William Soule on the west, John Mosher on the north, and Joseph Mosher and Stephen Wilcox on the east. All around these lots were familiar names – Philip Taber, William Corey, Ebenezer Tripp, James Tripp, Joseph Tripp, Abial Tripp, Peleg Tripp, John Tripp, Hugh Mosher. All these names in the Land Survey Books when the lots were laid out to the Dartmouth Proprietors in 1713 and 1714, and in other records as well. Abial Tripp married Ann Davis, probably Benjamin's sister, and the other Tripp men were Abial's brothers. Many of them were in my own ancestry. I had enough validation that the ancestral family of the Spirit Joe Tripp could have lived here, alongside the Davis family.

I looked at several other maps and documents that day at the library, which helped me glean a better understanding of the area and the successive generations of these families that occupied their homesteads. There was a copy of applications made to the Massachusetts Historical Commission in October 1988 for the purpose of placing two of the Davis houses on the state Historical Register. Both applications included photographs of the houses as they stood at that time. One of these houses, with a current address at the corner of Cornell Road and Main Road, was described as a store with a residence and was on a private lane off a rural road surrounded by woods and fields. The application stated it was built about 1792 and was an original part of the homestead of John Earl of Rhode Island which contained 289 acres and was surveyed and laid out to him in 1732. I believe this may have been the house and homestead of George Washington Davis Sr., and was originally the store that belonged to his father Benjamin and uncle William Davis.

The application for the other Davis house also gave an address on Cornell Road, just next door, and stated it was at the end of a laneway seven-tenths of a mile long off a rural road in fields and woods. It was built about 1800 with several additions onto the main house at later dates. The application stated, "Another Davis house resulting from subdivision of very extensive lands among subsequent generations." According to the application, pieces were taken from the original house to build this one. The laneway on which these houses sat was originally the principal roadway in the 1700s that joined Cornell Road to Main Road, the main road connecting Adamsville (in Little Compton), Rhode Island to Westport Point. This lane was probably the one referenced in the deed when George W.'s property was sold.

Bibliography – Works Cited and Referenced

"A 20-year-old skeleton..." *Springfield Republican*. Springfield, Massachusetts: July 20, 1876, page 6. Database, *Genealogy Bank*, Naples, Florida. Accessed July 18, 2018.

22nd Massachusetts Volunteer Infantry—Recreated. Website. Accessed June 6, 2019.

"Almshouse—Town Farm—Assistance to the Poor, Historic Documents." Scanned images of original documents. Website, *Town of Westport, Massachusetts*. Accessed July 2018 through July 2019.

"Ancestry Family Trees." Website, *Ancestry.com*. Online publication, Provo, Utah: Ancestry.com. Original data, public family trees files submitted by Ancestry members. Accessed July 2018 through July 2019.

"Annual Reports." Scanned images of original documents. Website, *Town of Westport, Massachusetts*. Accessed July 2018 through July 2019.

Archival Collections of the New Bedford Library Genealogical Department. New Bedford, Massachusetts.

Arnold, James N. *Vital record of Rhode Island, 1636-1850, first series, births, marriages and deaths: a family register for the people*, 21 volumes. Providence, Rhode Island: Narraganset Historical Publishing Co., 1891-1912.

Austin, James Osborne. *Genealogical Dictionary of Rhode Island*. Albany, New York: Printed by Joel Munsell's Sons, 1887.

Bollet, Alfred Jay, M.D. "Typhoid Fever." Website, *Civil War Rx*, The Source Guide to Civil War Medicine. Copyright 2011-2015, Jamco Films. Accessed August 9, 2018.

"Bristol County (Mass.) deed records, v. 1-556, (1686-1900) and (1686-1956) index—, 1686-1956." Microreproduction of original records in the registrar's office, Taunton, Mass. Website, *FamilySearch*. Salt Lake City, Utah: Genealogical Society of Utah, 1968.

"Bristol County, Massachusetts, Wills and Probate Records, 1635-1991." Database, *Ancestry.com*. Provo, Utah: Ancestry.com Operations, Inc., 2015. Original data: Bristol County Massachusetts Probate Court. Accessed July 2018.

Bristol County Sherriff's Office. Website. Accessed November 20, 2018.

"California Great Registers, 1866-1910." Database, *FamilySearch*. Posted 8 December 2017. Original Data: San Francisco County Clerk offices, California. Accessed August 9, 2018.

"California, Death Index, 1905-1939." Database, *Ancestry.com*. Provo, Utah: Ancestry.com Operations, Inc., 2013. Original data: California Department of Health and Welfare, California Vital Records. Accessed July 2018.

"California, Wills and Probate Records, 1850-1953." Database, *Ancestry.com*. Provo, Utah: Ancestry.com Operations, Inc., 2015. Original data: Superior Court, Solano County, California. Accessed July 19, 2018.

"The Civil War." Database, *National Park Service, United States Department of the Interior*. Last updated March 7, 2017. Accessed July 2018.

"Consolidated Lists of Civil War Draft Registration Records (Provost Marshal General's Bureau; Consolidated Enrollment Lists, 1863-1865)." Database, *Ancestry.com*. Provo, Utah: Ancestry.com Operations, Inc., 2010. Original data: National Archives and Records Administration (NARA); Washington, D.C. Accessed July 2018.

Crannell, Linda. Website, *The Poorhouse Story*. Copyright 2000-2014.

"Dartmouth, Early Town Records." Scanned images of original documents. Website, *Town of Westport, Massachusetts*. Accessed July 2018 through July 2019.

"Deeds." Scanned images of original documents. Website, *Town of Westport, Massachusetts*. Accessed July 2018 through July 2019.

DiBacco, Thomas V. "When Typhoid was Dreaded." *The Washington Post.* Washington, D.C.: January 25, 1994. Accessed August 9, 2018.

"Dorchester, Massachusetts Births, Marriages, Deaths, 1826-1844, Book III, Massachusetts, Town and Vital Records, 1620-1988." Database, *Ancestry.com.* Provo, Utah: Ancstry.com Operations, Inc., 2011. Original data: Town and City Clerks of Massachusetts; Holbrook Research Institute, Jay and Delene Holbrook.

Dorwart, Dr. Bonnie Brice. "Disease in the Civil War." Website, *Essential Civil War Curriculum.* Copyright 2010-2018, Virginia Center for Civil War Studies at Virginia Tech. Accessed August 9, 2018.

"Farm for Sale, Advertisement." *New Bedford Mercury.* New Bedford, Massachusetts: December 10, 1847. Database, *Genealogy Bank*, Naples, Florida. Accessed July 20, 2018.

The Field Notes of Benjamin Crane, Benjamin Hammond and Samuel Smith. New Bedford, Massachusetts: New Bedford Free Public Library, 1910.

"First Christian Church." Scanned images of original documents. Website, *Town of Westport, Massachusetts.* Accessed July 2018 through July 2019.

GPoppa, contributor. Find-A-Grave Memorial # 82925429, Memorial page for Pvt. Joseph H. Tripp (21 Dec 1843–18 Jun 1862), Beech Grove Cemetery, Westport, Bristol County, Massachusetts. Database and images, *Find-A-Grave.* Created January 3, 2012. Accessed July 18, 2018.

"Gravestone Search." Database and website, *Rhode Island Historical Cemetery Commission.* Accessed July 2018 through December 2018.

"Great Registers, 1866-1898." Database, *Ancestry.com.* Provo, Utah: Ancestry.com Operations, Inc., 2011. Original data: California State Library, California History. Accessed August 2018.

Hart, Irving and Col. Scott P. Hart. "From the Records of Constant Hart, of Tiverton, R.I." *New England Historical and Genealogical Register,* Volume 105, July 1951, page 213-217.

Historical and Archival Collection. Westport Public Library, Westport, Massachusetts.

"Historical Documents." Website, *Town of Westport, Massachusetts*. Digital copies of various town records. Accessed July 2018—June 2019.

"Historical Atlas Maps, Historical maps." Scanned images of original documents. Website, *Town of Westport, Massachusetts*. Accessed July 2018 through July 2019.

"Letters, Loss of Bark Milwood." *Whaleman's Shipping List and Merchants' Transcript*. New Bedford, Massachusetts: Tuesday morning, September 10, 1872, page 2. Database, *Genealogy Bank*, Naples, Florida. Accessed July 15, 2018.

"Letters and Journals of the Overseers 1848-1887." Scanned images of original documents. Website, *Town of Westport, Massachusetts*. Accessed July 2018 through March 2019.

"Licenses—Permits—Certificates." Scanned images of original documents. Website, *Town of Westport, Massachusetts*. Accessed July 2018 through July 2019.

Macomber, Andrew C. and Richard W. Wertz. *Westporters and the Civil War*. Booklet printed with a grant from the Helen E. Ellis Trust, administered by the Westport Arts Council, BayBanks Trustee, 1983.

"Maine, Marriage Records, 1713-1922." Database, *Ancestry.com*. Provo, Utah: Ancestry.com Operations, Inc., 2010. Original Data: Maine State Archives, Pre 1892 Delayed Returns. Accessed July 2018.

Massachusetts Soldiers, Sailors, and Marines in the Civil War, Volumes 1-8. Compiled and published by the Adjutant-General in accordance with chapter 475, Acts of 1899 and chapter 64, Resolves of 1930. 1930, Second edition 1937.

"Massachusetts, State Census, 1855 and 1865." Database, *Ancestry.com*. Provo, Utah: Ancestry.com Operations, Inc., 2014. Accessed July 2018. Original data: Massachusetts. 1855–1865 Massachusetts State Census [microform]. New England Historic Genealogical Society, Boston, Massachusetts.

"Massachusetts, Town and Vital Records, 1620-1988." Database, *Ancestry.com*. Provo, Utah: Ancestry.com Operations, Inc., 2011. Original Data: Massachusetts Town Vital Records Collection compiled by the New England Historic Genealogical Society. Accessed July 2018 through July 2019.

Pannoni, Paul A. and Dawn Manchester. *Biographies of Civil War Soldiers and Sailors of Westport, Massachusetts*. Alpharetta, Georgia: Mountain Arbor Press, 2018.

Pimental, D. J., contributor. Find A Grave Memorial # 77493660. Rural Cemetery, New Bedford, Massachusetts. Website, *Find-A-Grave*, database and images. Added October 2, 2011. Accessed August 17, 2018.

Praderio, Caroline. "It's Possible for a Person to Have Two Different Sets of DNA—Here's How It Happens." Website, *Science Alert*. Posted November 10, 2017. Accessed July 19, 2019.

"Proprietors Land Records." Scanned images of original documents. Website, *Town of Westport, Massachusetts*. Accessed July 2018 through July 2019.

Randall, George L. *Descendants of Joseph Tripp, Son of John Tripp*. Manuscript, collections of the New Bedford Library Genealogy Department, New Bedford, Massachusetts. New Bedford, Massachusetts: 1925.

Record of the Massachusetts volunteers, 1861-1865, 2 volumes. Published by the Massachusetts Adjutant General, under a resolve of the General Court. Boston: Wright & Potter, 1868-1870.

Rettner, Rachael. "3 Human Chimeras That Already Exist." Website, *Scientific American*. Posted August 8, 2016. Accessed July 19, 2019.

Sanborn, Frank B. "The Management of Almshouses in New England." A Presentation at the Eleventh Annual Session, National Conference of Charities and Correction, held at St. Louis, October 13-17, 1884. Website, *Social Welfare History Project*, Virginia Commonwealth University. Last modified July 18, 2017. Accesed August 18, 2018.

Savage, James. *The Genealogical Dictionary of the First Settlers of New England... in Four Volumes*. Boston, Massachusetts: Little, Brown and Company, 1862.

"Shipping List." *Whaleman's Shipping List and Merchants' Transcript*. New Bedford, Massachusetts: Tuesday morning, September 10, 1872, page 2. Database, *Genealogy Bank*, Naples, Florida. Accessed July 15, 2018.

"State Detective Oesting..." *Whaleman's Shipping List and Merchants' Transcript*. New Bedford, Massachusetts: Tuesday morning, July 26, 1876, page 2. Database, *Genealogy Bank*, Naples, Florida. Accessed July 18, 2018.

"Suicide in Westport." *Boston Herald*. Boston, Massachusetts: May 14, 1861, page 2.

"Tax Records and Other Information." Scanned images of original documents. Website, *Town of Westport, Massachusetts*. Accessed July 2018 through July 2019.

"Town Meeting." Scanned images of original documents. Website, *Town of Westport, Massachusetts*. Accessed July 2018 through July 2019.

"Town Meeting Auctions Poor Woman to Lowest Bidder." Website, *MassMoments, a project of Mass Humanities*. Accessed August 13, 2018.

"Town Records." Scanned images of original documents. Website, *Town of Westport, Massachusetts*. Accessed July 2018 through July 2019.

"U.S. City Directories, 1822-1995." Database, *Ancestry.com*. Provo, Utah: Ancestry.com Operations, Inc., 2011. Accessed August 2018.

"United States Census; 1850, 1860, 1870, 1880, 1900, 1910, 1920, Veteran's Schedule 1890." Databases, *Ancestry.com*. Provo, Utah: Ancestry.com Operations, Inc. Original Data: Records of the Bureau of the Census, National Archives, Washington, D.C. Accessed July 2018.

"United States Civil War and Later Pension Index, 1861-1917." Database, *FamilySearch*. Posted March, 24, 2016. Accessed July 2018.

"United Congregational Church, Little Compton, Rhode Island Vital Extracts 1636-1899, Vol. 8 Church Records: Member Lists, Baptisms,

Marriages, Deaths." Database, *Ancestry.com*. Provo, Utah: Ancestry.com Operations, Inc., 2014. Accessed August 17, 2018.

"Vital Records." Scanned images of original documents. Website, *Town of Westport, Massachusetts*. Accessed July 2018 through July 2019.

"Vital Records from The NEHGS Register." Database, *AmericanAncestors.org*. New England Historic Genealogical Society, 2014. (Compiled from articles originally published in *The New England Historical and Genealogical Register*.) Originally published Vol. 115, 1961, "Cemetery Inscriptions in Little Compton, Rhode Island." Accessed November 4, 2018.

"Westport Historic Private and Public Cemeteries." Database complied by the Cemetery Identification Group (CIG), working under the auspices of the Westport (Massachusetts) Historical Commission. Website, *Cemetery Department, Town of Westport, Massachusetts*. Accessed July through August 2018.

Westport Historical Society. Website. Westport, Massachusetts: copyright 2013. Accessed July 2018 through May 2019.

Whaling History, Connecting All Things Whaling. Website is a collaboration between Mystic Seaport and the New Bedford Whaling Museum. Core databases are the work of Judith Lund and Tim Smith. Copyright 2018. Accessed July 2018.

Wilbour, Benjamin Franklin. "John Tripp." *Little Compton Families*. Little Compton, Rhode Island: Little Compton Historical Society, 1967.

Wilbour, Benjamin Franklin and Waldo Chamberlain Sprague. "Cemetery Inscriptions in Little Compton, R. I." *The New England Historical and Genealogical Register*, Volume 115, October 1961, page 257-268.

About the Author

Susan E. Rogers lives with her partner Hardy in sunny St. Pete Beach, Florida, USA transplanted from Massachusetts. Her move was the catalyst to focus on her life-long ambition to write. She is a practicing psychic medium and Tarot reader, and her interests include genealogy and psychic spirituality, themes which often twist their way into her writing. She is a proficient practitioner of psychic and intuitive mediumship, adept at using such vehicles as Tarot, Runes, and Oracle readings to provide guidance and inspiration to her clients, with special abilities in past life readings and ancestor spirit guides. She holds certifications as Reiki Master Teacher, Akashic Records Practitioner, and Herbal Apprentice, and is also certified in Advanced Aromatherapy and Crystal Energy Healing.

Her first book in 2018, *Uncovering Norman – Proving the Former Life of a Ghost* was about her own psychic experiences receiving messages from the spirit world, and researching the life of a ghost named Norman to prove he once existed as a real person. An occult thriller, *Death in the Cards*, was published in 2023 and she is looking forward to her third book, to be published in the fall of 2024. She has a number of short stories published in print anthologies as well as literary and genre magazines.

Read more at www.susanerogers.com.